"As the indifference of our s *fewer and fewer people resp(* *gospel meetings. This has* .... *the need for personal evangelism. It is the one-on-one contacts of believers, establishing relationships with their neighbors, school-mates, and friends which proves most effective in seeing people evangelised in our day.*

"The volume which has been provided is an excellent resource for how to go about this work. Most of us feel ill at ease starting conversations about spiritual matters with total strangers. Some suggestive approaches will encourage you in this. The section on answering the honest and challenging questions which are presented to you will equip you with responses that are reasonable and valid.

"This publication does not promise "success" in personal evangelism, but it should awaken us to our responsibility and provide some very useful information to assist us in it."

A J Higgins

Everyday Evangelism

To Rachel
Happy Birthday

Lots of Love

Nathaniel & Leucianne

(23)

Everyday
Evangelism

Sharing the Gospel in Conversation

Paul McCauley & David Williamson

John Ritchie Publishing

40 Beansburn, Kilmarnock, Scotland

EVERYDAY EVANGELISM

Sharing the Gospel in Conversation

© 2018 Paul McCauley and David Williamson

ISBN-13: 978 1 912522 45 3

Cover design & typeset by Pete Barnsley (CreativeHoot.com)

Printed by Bell & Bain Ltd, Glasgow

Dedication

In memory of Ruth,
who shone with the beauty of her Saviour everyday.

To all the everyday evangelists, who build bridges, make
friendships, carry tracts, love souls, and seek the lost. May
God multiply your number and multiply your fruitfulness.

To Karen. You live out the gospel faithfully everyday
in our most precious mission field – our family,
(1 Sam. 30:24).

To Luke, Zach, Jacob and Levi. May you light up this dark
world as you light up my life.

To mum and dad. You taught me to not be impressed by
what the world offers. Your encouragement is a blessing.

To my Saviour. "May the Lamb that was slain receive the
reward of His suffering."

Paul McCauley

To Jennie. Your support, love, and friendship make the
journey sweet. Truly you are a gift from above (James 1:17).

To Anna and Caleb. You bring me joy every day. May the
Lord Jesus Christ become everything to you; and may you
grow to reflect His character and carry His gospel to your
own generation.

To my parents. For your spiritual counsel and care, and
your undying love, I give God thanks.

To the Lord of the harvest. For the glory of Your Name,
and the furtherance of Your Gospel, this book is written.

David Williamson

Acknowledgements

The desire to write *Everyday Evangelism*, while sparked by our own gospel work, was fanned into flame through opportunities we received to teach others what we had learned. It was maintained for four years by earnest Christians expressing their appreciation of the teaching, and reminding us that they awaited it in written form.

The local church who meet in Culloden Gospel Hall, Inverness, invited us to participate in the Highland Outreach Week on two occasions. This gave us the opportunity to formulate our thoughts into a structure suited to teaching, and put our ideas before an audience of zealous believers, both young and old. We are truly grateful for this opportunity. The feedback we received assured us of the potential value of this book.

Thanks must be given to our proofreading team: Johnny Caldwell, Ruth Chesney, Samuel Chesney, Leslie Craig, Stephen Grant, Douglas Mowat, Eunice Wilkie, Michael Wilkie, and Andrew Williamson. Their suggestions have undoubtedly improved this book tremendously. Douglas Mowat has also provided a very kind foreword. Also worthy of mention is David Newell who, while very busy with editorial work on other projects, cast his expert eye over part of the original draft of this book — providing helpful insight.

We are also truly grateful to Sandy Higgins who agreed to wear the editor's hat and, while busily engaged in his own ministry for the Lord, found time to apply his considerable skills to greatly enhance this book.

All of these "first gave themselves to the Lord, and then to us by the will of God" (2 Cor. 8:5).

Contents

Part 2: apologetics

FOREWORD

Everyday Evangelism – the title of this powerful book is a challenge in itself. Our secularised society – and perhaps a lack of spiritual courage – has meant that, for many Christians, evangelism is anything but *everyday*. And yet the very real need of our times is for a commitment to spreading the Gospel message on a daily basis. As has been said, we need a *spirit* of evangelism, not just a *spurt* of evangelism.

Commitment is, however, only part of the answer. Anyone who tries to engage in Gospel witness will soon find out that enthusiasm alone will not suffice. We also need to be *equipped*. This book has been written with a view to empowering a new generation of Christians to evangelise with confidence and purpose. The practical techniques taught by McCauley and Williamson are based on a thoroughly biblical foundation, and – unlike many volumes on evangelistic methods – they concentrate on presenting the Gospel message in a winsome and relevant manner, rather than on pressurising individuals into making decisions.

This is not an abstract academic thesis. McCauley and Williamson write with practical experience from the front line of Gospel witness. In this book they share with us the valuable lessons they have learnt on the job, and the result is that head, heart and hands are all engaged. We are benefitting from their first-hand experience.

If the principles of this book are blended with earnest prayer and a yielding to the leading of the Spirit of God, there can be no doubt that much will be accomplished. May the Lord use this volume to enthuse and equip us for *everyday evangelism*.

Douglas J H Mowat

Preface

Who would write a book about personal evangelism? Well, that's easy: it would be someone for whom sharing the gospel is as easy as breathing. Perhaps a charming extrovert whose natural choice of employment would be in sales and who could convince anyone that black is white. Right?

Wrong.

Some years ago, both of us were downhearted by our lack of ability to share the gospel in personal conversation. While engaged full time in gospel preaching and Bible teaching, we felt that we were not well equipped to open conversations with friends, neighbours, and strangers, and to wisely and winsomely communicate the gospel to them. This became a matter of earnest prayer and caused us to search the scriptures to see if this skill could be learned.

It can be.

Over the years we have visited many homes and distributed thousands of invitations to gospel meetings. However, some years ago, we decided to treat these visits as opportunities to share the gospel. Slowly but steadily, as we brought what we had learned in the study out to the street, we witnessed a massive transformation in our ability to speak of Christ to others.

As a result, we have been asked on a number of occasions to give practical teaching about personal evangelism. The interest of many young (and not-so-young) Christians has both surprised and greatly encouraged us. Some wanted the teaching to be preserved in a more permanent form — this book is the result. Our prayer is that the Lord will use it to equip believers to engage in everyday evangelism with family members, friends, colleagues, neighbours, and strangers.

Everyday Evangelism is in two parts: Part One deals with the nuts and bolts of conversation, and is intended to help you engage meaningfully with any unbeliever. Biblical techniques for opening and maintaining conversation, bringing conviction, responding to challenges, and communicating the gospel will be considered. Here, when the first person singular pronoun is used, David is the speaker.

Part Two considers many challenges that are often raised and gives practical guidance to help you answer them. These questions are arranged into the broad categories of scripture, science, suffering, salvation, and the Saviour. Paul is the speaker in this section.

While David has written Part One, and Paul has written Part Two, we have reviewed and contributed to each other's section and take full ownership for the content of the book.

It is important to stress that this book is not presented as the last word on personal evangelism. Neither of us is under the impression that we have "arrived" or that we have all the answers. However, we do believe that we have made progress on the journey, and are confident that we have *some* answers or this book would not have been written.

It is only right that we acknowledge the help we have received from many sources. Some of these have been referenced in the footnotes and in the recommended resources at the end of the book.

David Williamson & Paul McCauley

Part One:
Tactics

Introduction

Mary[1] arrived home to find a gospel leaflet on the floor of her little hallway. The text message I received from her that evening was encouraging:

Hi, I got your leaflet through my door. I have been having a feeling to become a Christian for a long time now. I just need to know how to go about it.

During that weekend, a group of young people had dropped five thousand gospel leaflets into houses in Belfast. This was the only response I would get.

After a little back-and-forth texting, I phoned her and we chatted for about twenty minutes. Although I was sure the eternal welfare of Mary was in the balance, I was calm as I conversed with her about God's way of salvation. Mary entered fully into the conversation, asking good questions about the reliability and relevance of the Bible, and about the simplicity and sufficiency of faith in Christ.

---

[1] All names of people with whom I have conversed have been changed for the sake of the individual's privacy.

By the grace of God, Mary trusted Christ as her Saviour during that conversation. She learned that faith in Christ alone was sufficient for her eternal blessing. She had never owned a Bible, she had never attended any form of gospel service, but she was on the way to heaven. I did not ask her to say a prayer, to sign a card, or to attend a meeting. Her conversion was a work of God, through faith in Christ. Mary was a "good ground" hearer (Mark 4:8). Little effort was required on my part; she listened willingly to the gospel and responded positively to Christ. It is an unspeakable privilege to be the bearer of cold water to a thirsty soul. In fact, if this had been the only person to trust Christ as a result of my work in the gospel, it would have made every effort worthwhile.

Many conversations with unbelievers about the gospel are not so encouraging. However, I have begun with a "success" story because I want to inspire you. I want you to envisage the joy of seeing souls saved through your personal witness for the Lord Jesus. I want you to be hungry to reach the lost with the gospel, because then the principles contained in this book will prove valuable to you.

The reason I remained perfectly calm in my conversation with Mary was that I had learned principles from the Bible applicable to personal evangelism – *principles that really work*. When the Lord said to Simon and Andrew, "Follow Me, and I will make you become fishers of men" (Mark 1:17), He confirmed that it was possible to learn to evangelise. My experience agrees with this. So, let's follow the Lord and learn from Him how to become fishers of men.

Chapter 1

EVANGELISM EXAMINED

Why this book? To some, a book giving guidance for evangelism may seem superfluous. Evangelism, so the argument goes, is the work of the evangelist, a man gifted by God for that work. It seems pointless to show evangelists how to evangelise – they already know. And it's a waste of time teaching other Christians to evangelise – it's not their job.

While this is the thinking of many, it is not the teaching of the New Testament. Certainly, some Christians are evangelists and others are not. However, no Christian is free from the responsibility to evangelise. This book is for those who would like to fulfil that responsibility.

In considering this subject, there are questions that must be answered. Rudyard Kipling wrote:

I keep six honest serving-men
(They taught me all I knew);
Their names are What and Why and When
And How and Where and Who.[2]

Let us employ these "honest serving-men" to examine our subject.

What is Evangelism?

This is a question to which we must find a good, biblical answer. The Greek word translated "evangelise" in the Bible simply means to "announce good news". However, when this word is used for the communication of the gospel message, it also stresses the purpose for which the good news is announced. An accurate definition of evangelism must take into account both the content of the message and the purpose of the messenger.

A Definition

Evangelism is telling sinners the gospel so that they may be saved. It is "an act of communication with a view to conversion".[3] The true message of good news is the biblical gospel, and the proper motive for its communication is the eternal salvation of souls.[4]

---

[2] Rudyard Kipling, The Elephant's Child, Just So Stories, 1902.
http://www.kiplingsociety.co.uk/poems_serving.htm.
[3] J. I. Packer, *Evangelism and the Sovereignty of God*, Inter-Varsity Press, 2010, p. 93.
[4] Undoubtedly there are other associated motives, e.g. the glory of God. However, I am defining from the human standpoint. We tell people the gospel, not only to be obedient to God's word, or to honour Christ, but because it is man's only hope for salvation from eternal damnation.

The message communicated must be the biblical gospel. Therefore, to evangelise well, we must ensure that we have a good knowledge of the gospel. We should not be content with a few well-known Bible verses, but should endeavour to familiarise ourselves with gospel doctrine as taught in scripture.

Shortly after I got saved I began to distribute gospel leaflets. This brought me into contact with many people who had false ideas and diverse ideologies. At first I found the experience very unsettling, but a careful study of Paul's letter to the Romans established me in the truth of the gospel. This in turn greatly increased my confidence in the message, enabling me to engage more fully with those who disagree.

The epistle to the Romans is "the most extensive, and most comprehensive exposition of the gospel found anywhere in Scripture,"[5] and is required reading for those who would evangelise. An accurate understanding of the gospel is basic to its correct communication to others.

We have defined evangelism as *telling sinners the gospel so that they may be saved*. Before we can communicate it, we must understand it.

A Distinction

Many do not evangelise because they have a wrong concept of evangelism. They hear evangelists speak of "seeing souls saved"' or "winning souls for Christ" and they conclude

---

[5.] Norman L. Geisler, *A Popular Survey of the New Testament*, Baker Books, 2007, p. 144.

that they cannot evangelise because they have never experienced this. Make no mistake, souls being saved is an intended *result* of evangelism, but it does not *define* it. We must make a clear distinction between the goal of evangelism and evangelism itself.

If evangelism is *telling sinners the gospel so that they may be saved*, then, if we have communicated the right message with the right motive, even if no positive results are evident, evangelism has still taken place.

> *Our job is not to convert people. It is to witness to Christ. Conversion isn't the mark of a successful witness — witnessing is. Think about a courtroom. Witnesses are there to tell the truth. That's successful witness. If the jury doesn't believe them, that's not their fault or failure. You have not failed if you explain the gospel and are rejected. You have failed if you don't try.*[6]

This is not to minimise the importance of results. When Paul wrote of his evangelistic activity, he showed himself deeply concerned for souls. In 1 Corinthians 9, he describes his outlook:

> *For though I am free from all men, I have made myself a servant to all, that I might win the more; and to the Jews I became as a Jew, that I might win Jews; to those who are under the law, as under the law, that I might win those who are under the law; to those who are without law, as without law (not being*

---

[6] Rico Tice, *Honest Evangelism*, The Good Book Company, 2015, p. 56.

> *without law toward God, but under law toward Christ), that*
> *I might win those who are without law; to the weak I became*
> *as weak, that I might win the weak. I have become all things*
> *to all men, that I might by all means save some. (vv. 19-22)*

Notice the repetition of "that I might win" (vv. 19, 20, 21, 22) and the conclusion "that I might by all means save some" (v. 22). Evidently Paul made personal sacrifices with a view to the salvation of souls. He was no unconcerned bystander as he preached the gospel. He ordered his life, and preached the gospel, to see souls saved.

Paul felt an obligation to tell people the gospel (Rom. 1:14) and was eager to discharge that responsibility (v. 15). However, he understood that God's power was required for salvation, and this power was not in the messenger but in the message (v. 16). Not only so, but the power of the gospel would only be effectual in the case of the sinner who believed the message. The message would not profit if not "mixed with faith in those who heard it" (Heb. 4:2). It is the sinner who must repent and believe, and it is God who saves. Results are not within the remit of the evangelist.

The Old Testament story of Naaman shows us the importance of a messenger (2 Kings 5:1-14). Naaman, a successful soldier, a courageous and celebrated commander of the Syrian army, had leprosy – an incurable disease at the time. In his household there was a servant girl who had been taken away from home and family during one of Naaman's military exploits in Israel. Knowing her new master's condition, she told of the "prophet who is in Samaria" who would "heal him of his leprosy" (2 Kings 5:3). She could not cure Naaman, neither could she command him to do anything, but she could communicate a message of hope to him.

This little maid illustrates well those who carry the message of salvation in Christ. We are messengers. We cannot save a soul, neither can we make anyone believe the gospel. We are not responsible for either of these matters. Our role is to deliver the message which alone provides hope for the world.

It is liberating to realise your limits. You cannot save, but you can tell what you know – you can *tell sinners the gospel so that they may be saved.*

Why do personal evangelism?

The need to evangelise is evident. Our friends, neighbours, and family members face eternal banishment from God and unending punishment in hell if they do not trust in Christ. But why do *personal* evangelism?

The Logic of Love

Without personal evangelism, many will not hear the gospel and will remain exposed to the righteous wrath of God.

Some believe that those who do not hear the gospel are exempt from judgment.[7] When Paul, however, establishes

---

[7.] A little thought will show how this is impossible. The gospel is good news; but if everyone who has not heard it is saved, and most who have heard it are lost, it seems like bad news. What encouragement is this for pioneer evangelism if, *before* we go everyone is safe, and *after* we go many are lost? For more on this subject see the relevant section in chapter 10.

the guilt of humanity before God (Rom. 1:18-3:20), a mainstay of his reasoning is that man is not *ignorant*, therefore he is not *innocent*. Those who haven't heard the gospel have the witness of Creation (1:18-32), Conscience (2:1-16) and (in some cases) Covenantal privilege (2:17-3:8). Their rejection of divine revelation therefore leaves them "guilty before God" (3:19).[8]

General revelation, when rejected, brings about a person's righteous condemnation. However, the gospel alone "is the power of God to salvation for everyone who believes" (Rom. 1:16). Thankfully, the word of God makes clear that a person who responds correctly to the revelation they have been given will receive further light. No true seeker will be left in the dark.[9] However, none will be saved without the gospel (cf. Rom. 10:14).

It is important to grasp this fact: God gives us no encouragement in His word to believe that anyone will be saved without hearing the gospel. We know that many people will never hear a formal public proclamation of the gospel; how then can they hear this indispensable message? One answer is personal evangelism.

Personal evangelism is a New Testament method of reaching people who would not otherwise hear the gospel. The apostle Paul recognised this. When he was under house

---

[8.] This does not include those children who are too young to be held accountable for actions they do not understand to be wrong. Nor do we include people with learning disabilities which seriously impair the ability to rationally consider the information provided.

[9.] Cornelius is an example of such a man. He was earnest and sincere before God. However, before he was saved the gospel was needed (Acts 10:1-11:18). The Ethiopian Eunuch is another example (Acts 8:26-40).

arrest in Rome and some thought gospel progress would be restricted, he assured them that the opposite was true. "But I want you to know, brethren, that the things which happened to me have actually turned out for the furtherance of the gospel" (Php. 1:12). Paul viewed his imprisonment, and the close proximity it gave him to others, as the means, under God, by which the gospel reached new territory. As a result of Paul's personal evangelism, a path was cut all the way into Caesar's household (4:22).

People need the gospel, and personal evangelism delivers what they need. Let us not forget that we are all responsible to love our neighbours. Just as love would constrain us to throw a lifeline to a drowning man, so genuine love will motivate us to use the means at our disposal to rescue souls from a fate far worse than drowning.

The Demands of Duty

Doing personal evangelism is simple obedience to the exhortations of the word of God. The last few verses of Matthew's Gospel contain the Great Commission in which the Lord encouraged His disciples to faithfully witness for Him in His bodily absence.

> All authority has been given to Me in heaven and on earth. Go therefore and make disciples of all the nations, baptizing them in the name of the Father and of the Son and of the Holy Spirit, teaching them to observe all things that I have commanded you; and lo, I am with you always, even to the end of the age. (Matt. 28:18-20)

Some believe that this commission was intended only for the apostles. However, that interpretation is not tenable for two reasons. First, the apostles are instructed to teach their converts "to observe all things that I have commanded you". Therefore, if this commission is included in what the Lord *commanded* His apostles, then they must *communicate* it to their converts. So, the commission is to be observed not only by apostles, but by Christians. Secondly, the promise given by the Lord was that "I am with you always, even to the end of the age". If this promise was only made to the apostles, and not through them to their converts, to what does the "end of the age" refer? Is the Lord not promising His presence with all those who faithfully communicate His truth from apostolic times until His return? Here is a clear exhortation to personal evangelism; for while not all believers can preach, yet all should evangelise.

Another occasion of commissioning is found in Acts 1. The apostles gathered around the Lord Jesus again and asked concerning the timing of the restoration of the kingdom to Israel. The Lord responded:

> *It is not for you to know times or seasons which the Father has put in His own authority. But you shall receive power when the Holy Spirit has come upon you; and you shall be witnesses to Me in Jerusalem, and in all Judea and Samaria, and to the end of the earth. (vv. 7-8)*

To whom did the Lord communicate these words? *First* He spoke to the apostles, but necessarily *through them to*

Christians in general. We accept that it is not for us to know the times or the seasons, and we rejoice that the power of the Holy Spirit is ours because of Pentecost. How then can we refuse to accept that we also have responsibility to witness "to the end of the earth"?

In the epistles of the New Testament, this duty to evangelise is re-emphasised. Paul refers to believers as "ambassadors for Christ" through whom God appeals, and by whom Christ implores people to be "reconciled to God" (2 Cor. 5:20). He instructs us to "walk in wisdom toward those who are outside, redeeming the time" and to let our "speech always be with grace, seasoned with salt, that you may know how you ought to answer each one" (Col. 4:5-6). Peter likewise exhorts suffering believers, "sanctify the Lord God in your hearts, and always be ready to give a defense to everyone who asks you a reason for the hope that is in you, with meekness and fear" (1 Pet. 3:15). These exhortations encourage us to engage in meaningful, spiritually beneficial, conversations with unbelievers.

Christians in the first century evidently understood that these exhortations applied to them, for personal evangelism was not only the common practice of the Lord Jesus and the apostles, but of early Christians in general, as is clear from a cursory reading of the book of Acts.

As Christians, we are motivated by a variety of reasons. We read God's word, both out of love to the Author, and in obedience to His authority. Love and a sense of duty intertwine to make us responsible in this basic discipline of Christian life. This is also true of prayer, worship, and service. Personal evangelism should be considered in the same way: love and duty are twisted together, and are the great motivations for reaching the lost with the gospel.

Who should be involved?

Closely linked with the necessity for personal evangelism is the question of who should be involved in it. Only a few can be involved in public preaching, but almost everyone can converse with their friends and neighbours about the Lord.

It is vital to see that evangelism was never meant to be left to "professionals". Confirmation of this is found in Paul's letter to the Christians at Ephesus. The ascended Christ "gave some to be apostles, some prophets, some evangelists, and some pastors and teachers, for the equipping of the saints for the work of ministry" (Eph. 4:11-12). Evangelists should be "equipping … the saints".[10] These equipped believers *all* should engage in the "work of ministry". While the evangelist should certainly evangelise, he must also train up other believers to carry out this necessary work.[11]

The participation of all the early Christians in personal evangelism is verified by Luke. Writing of an occasion of great persecution against the church in Jerusalem, he

---

[10] In the scriptures the term "saints" never differentiates one group of Christians from another. It is one of many labels given by the Holy Spirit to all believers. Apparently, then, all Christians should be involved in announcing the good news of Christ to others.

[11] J. P. Moreland goes so far as to say "the test of the gift of evangelism is not how effective you are at winning others to Christ, but rather, your track record at training others to evangelise", *Love Your God With All Your Mind: The Role of Reason in the Life of the Soul*, NavPress, 2nd ed. 2012, loc. 3362.

records: "those who were scattered went everywhere preaching the word" (Acts 8:4). The scattered people he identifies as "the church" (vv. 1, 3). Luke writes not of apostles nor evangelists, but simply of *Christians* – all of whom engaged in evangelism.

The same pattern is repeated in Acts 11:

Now those who were scattered after the persecution that arose over Stephen traveled as far as Phoenicia, Cyprus, and Antioch, preaching the word to no one but the Jews only. But some of them were men from Cyprus and Cyrene, who, when they had come to Antioch, spoke to the Hellenists, preaching the Lord Jesus. And the hand of the Lord was with them, and a great number believed and turned to the Lord. (Acts 11:19-21)

These gospel labourers are simply described as "men from Cyprus and Cyrene". They were neither apostles nor evangelists yet they were "preaching the word" (v. 19) and "preaching the Lord Jesus" (v. 20). The repeated word "preaching" is a translation of two distinct Greek words. First, these believers were *speaking* the word and, in their personal conversations, they *announced the good news* of the Lord Jesus. God blessed their evangelistic endeavours with a great harvest of souls.

For early Christians, telling their peers about the gospel was common practice. They viewed the Great Commission not as an option to be considered, but as a command to be obeyed.[12] How do we compare with the fervour, courage, and commitment of these early Christians? James Boccardo summarised the problem: "I've noticed something different about people in the New Testament: they weren't silent about their faith".[13] Are we disobedient to the example and exhortations of scripture concerning the essential task of evangelism?

Where should I evangelise?

Knowing my responsibility to evangelise, where should I do it? What are the limits of my responsibility: where do I start, and where do I stop?

Where should I start?

The book of Acts has many lessons for those who would evangelise. We have seen from Acts 8 that "those who were scattered went everywhere preaching the word" (v. 4). This gives some insight into where we should start.

The Greek word for "scattered" is used for sowing seed. A great persecution had arisen, undoubtedly instigated by the devil. However, while the devil was *scattering* the Christians by means of persecution, God was also sovereignly using the same means to *sow* the Christians throughout the Roman Empire.

Up until this time in the history of the church, many believers had remained at Jerusalem. The Lord had made clear that the gospel was to spread much farther than

---

[12.] Hudson Taylor, source unknown.

[13.] James Boccardo, *Unsilenced: How to Voice the Gospel*, CrossBooks, 2012, p. 5.

Jerusalem – they were to be His witnesses "in Jerusalem, and in all Judea and Samaria, and to the end of the earth" (Acts 1:8). But rather than spread out with the gospel, many early Christians (including the apostles) remained at Jerusalem until persecution forced them to leave. What seemed like a negative circumstance caused by satanic opposition was overruled by God. What appeared as defeat for the Christians was a strategic victory for Christianity. All was under divine control.

The Christians were sown throughout the Roman Empire. When seed is sown, it produces fruit where it lands. God intended that His people would bring forth gospel fruit just where He placed them. He distributed them widely; He placed them strategically; and they evangelised where they were sown. Undoubtedly many would have wanted to remain in Jerusalem, but circumstances forced the change. God wasn't arranging things as they would have desired, but He was working to a plan of His own design, for the furtherance of His purpose – the spread of the gospel.

Perhaps you wonder why you are where you are. You would like to change your job, your neighbourhood, or your friends. In the future, circumstances may change. But in the present, wherever you are, God intends you to further His purpose in reaching the lost. "Your neighbour lives down your street because God put him there. Your colleague at work sits at the next desk to you because God sat him there".[14] Seek to produce fruit where He has sown you.

[14.] Tice, *Honest Evangelism*, p. 49.

Where should I stop?

The scope of the Commission shows that there need be no stopping. The Lord's command comes with "all authority" and instructs us to make disciples of "all the nations" (Matt. 28:18-20).

Very often we are blinkered by social status, religious persuasion, cultural differences, or racial prejudices. The gospel knows no such barriers. The apostle Paul felt an obligation to people of every background: "I am a debtor both to Greeks and to barbarians, both to wise and to unwise" (Rom. 1:14).

The early Christians, most of whom were Jews, found it difficult at the beginning to reach out to the Gentiles. There were reasons for this, some of which must have sounded plausible. However, because they overcame their narrow-mindedness, the book of Acts records the advance of the gospel from the religious centre of Judaism in Jerusalem, to the pagan centre of world power in Rome.

In Genesis we learn that Shem, Ham, and Japheth are the progenitors of the world population. By these three sons of Noah the nations were "divided on the earth after the flood" (Gen. 10:32). In Acts 8-10, Luke records the salvation of three men, descendants of Ham, Shem, and Japheth. An Ethiopian (chapter 8), a Jew (chapter 9), and a Roman (chapter 10) trusted Christ and received salvation. By this the Spirit of God makes clear the universal character of God's gospel.

We need no extra-biblical nudge from God to engage in personal evangelism because the Great Commission gives us sufficient authority to take the gospel anywhere.[15] The book of Acts does, however, record instances of special communication from heaven before evangelism took place. In Acts 8, for example, Philip was directed by an angel and by the Spirit of God (vv. 26-29), and in Acts 10, Peter received a vision. It would be foolish to say that God *cannot* work in this way today, however it is certainly not normal practice, nor should it be necessary for us. We have seen in Acts 11 that the gospel progressed *without apostles or evangelists.* It is also important to see that it progressed *without special communication from heaven.* Men of Cyprus and Cyrene (vv. 19-21) spread the word simply on the grounds of the Great Commission.

Prior to this time, it was common to only evangelise the Jews (v. 19). However, the efforts of the men of Cyprus and Cyrene resulted in the gospel being told to pagan Greeks (v. 20). This was a momentous step forward, and yet it was a step of simple obedience to the Lord's command. What authority did these "ordinary" men have to evangelise the Greeks? All they had was the command of the Lord to "make disciples of all the nations" and they reckoned His word was enough. God blessed their efforts and the "hand of the Lord was with them, and a great number believed and turned to the Lord" (v. 21).

God is intent on world evangelisation. There is no place to stop. There is no border we should not cross, no culture

---

[15.] I do not say that no one has ever received such a nudge but that we do not need it. Some insist that they need a personal, individually-tailored word from the Lord before they should evangelise; this is tantamount to saying that God's word, interpreted contextually, is insufficient to direct our lives.

we should not invade with the gospel, no heart we should not challenge with the claims of Christ. If the Lord has all authority, and the message is for all nations, then we are duty bound to spread the gospel wherever we can.

When should I evangelise?

This question is not as simple as it may sound. The reason for the difficulty is that two important features of evangelism must be balanced: urgency and strategy.

The need for Urgency

Evangelising is urgent because there is a vast target of people, and a limited time to reach them. If everyone is a target for the gospel, and there are no people for whom the gospel is unnecessary, then the number of people the gospel must reach is, at present, over seven billion. The sheer immensity of this number should spur us to evangelise.

Furthermore, time is running out for each person. On average, over 150,000 people die every day -- over one hundred every minute. The staggering implication is that multitudes of people leave earth for heaven or hell every day and for them there is no return. For those who arrive in hell, there is no escape from their suffering, no end to their sorrow. They are eternally under God's judgment, separated from His presence, enduring righteous punishment for their sins.

This should motivate us; urgency is certainly required! Aligned with this solemn need, however, is:

The need for Strategy

The burning need for evangelism should not cause us to take leave of our senses and rush out into the street shouting the gospel at everyone we meet.[16] Our passion for souls should not make us rude, obnoxious, or impossible to live with. While we should view people as souls bound for eternity, we must understand that winning them for Christ is a complex matter. What may stir one person to realise the urgency of salvation may cause another person to view us as rude, mad, or both.

Thankfully, we are not left to ourselves: the Bible provides us with the help we need. The Lord's many discussions with individuals show that He did not force conversations but guided and controlled them. He did not compel people to listen to Him, nor did He chase after those who refused Him.

When a rich young ruler came running to Jesus and, kneeling before Him, cried, "Good Teacher, what shall I do that I may inherit eternal life?" all looked promising. He was earnest and his question was relevant. However, the conclusion of the story is that he "went away sorrowful" (Mark 10:17-22). "Jesus, looking at him, loved him" (v. 21), but He did not chase after him. This is an important principle. If we are wise, we will boldly proclaim the gospel, but we will not make a nuisance of ourselves in doing so. Being aggressive and pushy with people is often, in the long term, counter-productive.

[16.] Although this would be preferable to complete lethargy.

Therefore, while we recognise the urgency of the message, we also respect the dignity of individuals. We believe that they have the capacity to make choices, and we respect the choices they make. Simply put, we control our emotions and direct our actions to maximise our usefulness for God and our impact upon others. As the proverb states: "he who wins souls is wise" (Prov. 11:30).

In the prologue of his letter to the Philippian church, Paul recorded his deep appreciation of the believers. He valued their love for the gospel and their love for him. He could see so much that was to their credit, but he did not cease to pray for them. He desired that their "love may abound still more and more in knowledge and all discernment" (Php. 1:9). If their love was a river, Paul desired that it become deeper and deeper. However, he made clear that the river of their love should flow between the banks of knowledge and discernment. Therefore, in all our gospel activity, our sincere love for the lost should be guided by wisdom from above.

One of the most helpful pieces of advice I received about evangelism was not to forget that God is sovereign.[17] If I think everything depends on me, I will become pushy and obnoxious. However, if I believe that God gives opportunities, and that I am a small link in the chain, I can trust Him to continue working with a person after I have left him. This means that I can grasp the opportunity I'm

---

[17.] I am not arguing here for a theological position but simply asserting the control God has, and exercises, in the world. I believe that sovereignty is basic to who God is, just as I believe that free will is basic to what man is.

given without feeling the need to force the conversation in an unnatural way. Greg Koukl explains:

> *Since I know I play only one part in a larger process of bringing anyone to the Lord, I'm comfortable taking smaller steps towards that end.*[18]

Koukl's point must be grasped for, when applied correctly, it allows conversations to happen which, while not strictly evangelistic, have an evangelistic purpose.

Let us suppose that you have a conversation on a plane. The person seated beside you asks why you are travelling, and you tell him you are on the way to a Bible conference. He doesn't seem very impressed, so you ask, "What are your thoughts about the Bible?" His answer is that he believes the Bible to be a collection of myths and legends, full of unscientific claims, and riddled with contradictions. You have little time left on the flight but for the remainder of your time you give reasons why you believe the Bible to be trustworthy. You show him some of the fulfilled prophecies of scripture and, before you know it, the plane has landed and your time is up. You separate, perhaps never to meet again.

You may leave the conversation thinking, "I didn't really tell him the whole gospel," and you may be right. But does that make the conversation worthless? Not at all. If you have brought a person one step closer to the truth, your time was well spent. To quote Koukl again, "All I want to do is put

---

[18.] Gregory Koukl, *Tactics: A Game Plan for discussing your Christian Convictions*, Zondervan, 2009, p. 38.

a stone in someone's shoe. I want to give him something worth thinking about, something he can't ignore".[19]

While we may feel uncomfortable with the notion that a conversation without the gospel can be profitable, the conversations of the Lord Jesus are full of such occasions.[20] The Lord spoke to people about the subjects they raised with Him; He answered the questions they levelled at Him, and often the conversation went no further. In *The Pilgrim's Progress*, after Hopeful and Christian had spoken to Ignorance, they walked ahead and discussed what more they should say: "Shall we talk further with him, or outgo him at present, and so leave him to think of what he hath heard already, and then stop again afterwards, and see if by degrees we can do any good to him?" Hopeful concludes:

> *Let Ignorance a little while now muse*
> *On what is said, and let him not refuse*
> *Good counsel to embrace ...*[21]

A starving man is not always best served with a five-course meal. Sometimes it is wise to take time and give people what they can stomach so that, when they have digested the information, they may seek more.

Urgency is needed, but strategy is also required. The need of sinners should spur me to action, but the nature of God should preserve me from panic.

[19.] Ibid., p. 38.
[20.] See chapter 4.
[21.] John Bunyan, *The Pilgrim's Progress*, Christian Focus Publications, 2005, p. 132.

How should I go about it?

This is the question with which the remainder of this book is concerned. The example of the Lord Jesus and of the early Christians will provide us with the answer we need. Our intention in this book is not primarily to *exhort* you to evangelise, but to *equip* you to engage in profitable gospel conversations with friends, neighbours, colleagues, and strangers.

Possibly no incident in the life of the Lord Jesus gives greater guidance for personal evangelism than the story of His conversation with the woman of Samaria. This cross-culture conversation is a delight to read, and a greater delight to examine from the standpoint of personal evangelism.

For the first part of this book, we intend to consider the following subjects:

1. Making Conversation
2. Bringing Conviction
3. Facing Challenges
4. Preaching Christ

Under each of these headings, the Lord's conversation with the woman of Samaria will be examined. We will also make reference to many other portions of scripture as they shed further light on our subject. We want to communicate *scriptural* principles for personal evangelism. If we succeed, this book will prove beneficial in whatever sphere personal evangelism is conducted. While application to individual circumstances may require wisdom, the principles of God's word will hold good.

Chapter 2

MAKING
CONVERSATION

The most difficult part of any evangelistic conversation is making it happen. Many of us would be happy to answer questions put to us by non-believers. However, the idea of taking the initiative and opening a discussion with someone about salvation is enough to make us break out in a cold sweat.

I am very familiar with this feeling. For some years I worked in an insurance company, sharing an office with many people. While I sincerely longed to tell these people the gospel, and prayed often for their salvation, I struggled to start conversations. The office building was in the centre of a city and I spent my lunch breaks open-air gospel preaching and handing out gospel leaflets. I wanted my colleagues to walk past and to hear the gospel from me in that setting.

Was that not more frightening than opening a conversation with a friend? No, it wasn't. I found it less demanding to preach to people at a distance than to converse with people face-to-face. My fear of evangelising my friends and colleagues was so great that it was easier to hand out gospel tracts randomly to strangers.

Thankfully, much of that irrational fear has gone. That is not to say that I have no fears as I enter into dialogue with friends or strangers, but a little equipping has gone a long way.

Consider the Lord's conversation with the Samaritan woman.

What led to the Conversation?

Therefore, when the Lord knew that the Pharisees had heard that Jesus made and baptized more disciples than John (though Jesus Himself did not baptize, but His disciples), He left Judea and departed again to Galilee. But He needed to go through Samaria. (John 4:1-4)

The Lord was travelling from Judea towards Galilee and He "needed to go through Samaria" (v. 4). This was not a geographical necessity, nor was it the conventional route taken by the Jews. In fact, most Jews of Jesus' time would have avoided going through Samaria as the Samaritans were considered racially and religiously abhorrent. Orthodox Jews would have travelled east to the Jordan river, and then travelled northward through the Jordan valley to Galilee.

Why was it essential for the Lord to pass through Samaria? Was He in a hurry? The quickest route from

Judea to Galilee was through Samaria but the Lord stayed in Samaria for two days (vv. 40, 43). Evidently He wasn't pushed for time.

The Lord went through Samaria to evangelise the Samaritans. The Lord lived an intentional life, ordering His days around the fulfilment of His Father's will and the blessing of souls. He had goals before Him, ambitions which He would ensure were realised. He knew that He must "be lifted up" (John 3:14), and He deliberately took every step of obedience to God's will that led to that goal. Likewise, the Lord knew that, to reach the Samaritans, He must go through Samaria.

The first step towards doing personal evangelism is being intentional about it. Deliberate personal decisions must be made. It is worth asking yourself whether you live an intentional life or not. Do you have definite spiritual ambitions? Do you have priorities that resemble those of the Saviour? Do you order your life to fulfil God's will and to reach the lost?

Here are three suggestions to help you be intentional about personal evangelism:

1. Be Prayerful

"Prayer is that apparently useless activity, without which all activities are useless".[22] While the Lord knew exactly who He would meet in Samaria, we do not have such knowledge. How then can we be sure that our life is arranged in such

---

[22.] Simon Barrington-Wood, cited in Tice, *Honest Evangelism*, p. 98.

a way as will further God's saving purpose by bringing us into contact with sinners? The answer is prayer.

God arranges our circumstances and the contacts we meet in life. If we pray for His guidance, we can trust Him to bring across our path individuals with whom we can converse. How often do you ask the Lord to open opportunities for personal evangelism? How often have you prayed for God to bring circumstances into the lives of your friends, neighbours, and work colleagues that would cause them to seek Him? The sentiment of W. H. Houghton should be expressed to God daily:

> *Lead me to some soul today,*
> *O teach me, Lord, just what to say;*
> *Friends of mine are lost in sin,*
> *And cannot find their way.*
> *Few there are who seem to care,*
> *And few there are who pray;*
> *Melt my heart, and fill my life,*
> *Give me one soul today.*[23]

2. Be Prepared

Another essential component to being intentional about personal evangelism is preparation.

I was asked on one occasion to give a presentation to several insurance brokers who were visiting our company offices. A new product had been released and we wanted to

---

[23.] W. H. Houghton, *Lead Me To Some Soul Today*, 1936, renewed 1964, Hope Publishing Company.

encourage the brokers to sell it for us. Our product was one of many on the market at the time.

If you had been asked to give that presentation, what would you have done? First, you would get to know your product. Then you would compare it with what was on offer from other companies, to enable you to quickly distinguish your product from theirs. You might also think of potential questions the brokers might raise, and of suitable answers to those questions. Time would certainly be spent in preparation before giving the presentation.

My preparation meant that I could speak confidently about our product. In fact, it had left me enthusiastic about what we had to offer, and well equipped for the questions that would follow.

In the same way, time spent preparing to share the gospel with others is never time wasted. Gaining a fuller knowledge of gospel doctrine, memorising Bible verses, learning how to answer common objections, and being aware of how the true gospel differs from all other "gospels", will equip you to engage in many profitable discussions.

One of the greatest barriers to evangelism is fear. This fear often springs from an inability to explain or defend the gospel. This need not be. A little dedicated study will give you knowledge of your subject and the challenges people raise.

3. Be Proactive
Benjamin Franklin said, "Tell me and I forget. Teach me

and I remember. Involve me and I learn,"[24] and he wasn't wrong. The intention of this book is to teach you some guidelines for personal evangelism which we have found very beneficial; however, you will only *learn* them when you involve yourself in this work. A person needs to be in the water before they learn to swim, and progress will depend upon further time spent in the water. Having prayed and prepared, just do it – and *keep* doing it.

Because I am engaged full time in gospel work, I often have opportunity to share the gospel in conversation. However, there are occasions when for some months, through Bible-teaching commitments, involvement in personal evangelism is greatly reduced and I soon get rusty. The cut and thrust of conversation is where we learn the practice of conversational evangelism, and I would encourage you to involve yourself regularly in this work.

Why not commit to distributing gospel tracts on a city street once in the week? Determine before you go out that you will not be content with thrusting the tracts into the hands of passing people, but that you will attempt to engage them in conversation. Or, why not involve yourself in your local church gospel activities to a fuller degree, giving out invitations to gospel meetings? Determine to use the opportunity to open gospel conversations. Better still,

---

[24.] This may have been derived from a saying by an ancient Chinese philosopher Xun Kuang: "Not having heard something is not as good as having heard it; having heard it is not as good as having seen it; having seen it is not as good as knowing it; knowing it is not as good as putting it into practice" (*Xunzi, Ruxiao*, Ch. 11, John Knoblock trans.).

why not set yourself goals to introduce the message of the gospel to each of your unsaved friends/colleagues?

Philip the evangelist is a good example of this proactive mindset. It appears that on his own initiative he "went down to the city of Samaria and preached Christ to them" (Acts 8:5). However, he was also a man living in prayerful dependence upon God, and the Lord arranged for him to cross the path of the man from Ethiopia. Evidently he was sufficiently prepared to make full use of the opportunity provided, for, when the Ethiopian recognised the need for someone to guide him, Philip was ready and able to begin at the same scripture and tell him of the Lord Jesus.

If you pray regularly for opportunities, prepare thoroughly to take advantage of those opportunities, and proactively seek them, you will undoubtedly be involved in more evangelistic conversations.

A General Principle

Before we consider the detail of the Lord's conversation, it is necessary to notice the flow of it. The Lord commences the conversation by referring to the everyday circumstance of the woman (v. 7) and concludes with a revelation of Himself (v. 26).

Here is an overriding principle which governs evangelistic conversation: we must get our start from the sinner and set our sights on the Saviour. *Our conversation must make a connection (with the sinner) and have a direction (to the Saviour).*

Evidence of this abounds in the practice of the Lord and the apostles. Finding a man reading his Bible, Philip "beginning at this Scripture, preached Jesus to him" (Acts 8:35). When among Jews in the synagogues, Paul "reasoned with them from the Scriptures, explaining and demonstrating that the Christ had to suffer and rise again from the dead, and saying, 'This Jesus whom I preach to you is the Christ.'" (17:2-3). On Mars Hill among idolaters, he began with their devotions to the unknown God whom he identified as the Creator, and concluded with Christ risen from the dead (17:22-34). As Green puts it, "Jews were approached via the Old Testament; pagans, it seems, through the light of natural revelation, leading on to Christ."[25]

All were careful to obtain their starting point in the circumstance and understanding of their listeners, and to lead them from that point to the truth about Christ. We should follow this example.

How was the Contact made?

So He came to a city of Samaria which is called Sychar, near the plot of ground that Jacob gave to his son Joseph. Now Jacob's well was there. Jesus therefore, being wearied from His journey, sat thus by the well. It was about the sixth hour. A woman of Samaria came to draw water. Jesus said to her, "Give Me a drink." For His disciples had gone away into the city to buy food. (John 4:5-8)

[25.] Michael Green, *Evangelism in the Early Church*, Eagle, Inter Publishing Service, 1995, p. 152.

Here the Lord opened a conversation with a person who did not know Him, a woman who had never met Him before.

A popular Jewish saying from the time forbad contact between even the *shadows* of Jews and Gentiles.[26] This shows why it was necessary for the Lord to commence the conversation. From the standpoint of the woman, everything was against this conversation taking place. She was of a different race and religion. He was a Jew, she was a Samaritan, and the Samaritans were despised by the Jews.

Also, many Jewish men started each day with a prayer thanking God that they were not a Gentile but a Jew, not a slave but free, not a woman but a man.[27] This formed another barrier for she was of a different gender to the Lord. For a Jewish man to speak to any woman in a public place was considered unacceptable. Even if the woman was his wife or mother, daughter or sister, he would not converse publicly with her.

Clearly, the likelihood of this woman opening a conversation with a person whom she perceived to be antagonistic to her race and religion and contemptuous of her gender and lifestyle was very slim. Knowing this, the Lord, in gracious love, took the initiative. *If He had not done so, the conversation would never have taken place.*

There is an important lesson for us to learn here. We are responsible, not only to answer challenges and questions concerning our faith, but (on occasion) to open the conversation. Many people who are spiritually dissatisfied

---

[26] Jerram Barrs, *Learning Evangelism from Jesus*, Crossway, 2009, pp. 36-37.
[27] Ibid., pp. 38-39.

will never approach us because they have wrong perceptions about Christians and Christianity. Some feel there will be no welcome for them personally, or no understanding of their lifestyle, or no acceptance of their questions. Therefore, to bridge that gap, we need to open conversations.

The method used by the Lord was to make a simple request, "Give Me a drink" (v. 7). This request:

- Treated her with dignity. The Lord's words communicated an attitude of respect. He was not only willing to converse with her, He was willing to receive from her. He treated her as a social equal.

- Demolished her preconceptions. As a Samaritan woman, and (probably) a renowned sinner, she did not expect this Jew to converse with her at all. His willingness to do so showed that He did not allow cultural and religious differences to impact His valuation of her worth.

- Removed her defences. A man who requests assistance does not appear dangerous. While the Lord would later challenge her actions and her understanding, at this point He did not appear as a threat at any level. The conversation commenced with her still firmly within her comfort zone.

The Lord's approach contains tremendous lessons for all who desire to open conversations with unbelievers about the gospel. To truly engage with people we must do as the Lord did. We must show respect, demolish preconceptions, and put the person at ease.

One method often practised in scripture to achieve these ends is to adopt the role of *questioning* rather than *preaching*.

Why should we ask Questions?

God is the first evangelist in scripture. At creation, Adam and Eve lived in perfect harmony with their Creator, but Genesis 3 records the entrance of sin into the world. Immediately following this sad occasion, Adam and Eve "heard the sound of the LORD God walking in the garden in the cool of the day" and responded to the voice of God by hiding "from the presence of the LORD God among the trees of the garden" (v. 8).

How did the Lord approach them? How did He draw them out from the shadows into the light?

> *Then the LORD God called to Adam and said to him, "Where are you?" So he said, "I heard Your voice in the garden, and I was afraid because I was naked; and I hid myself." And He said, "Who told you that you were naked? Have you eaten from the tree of which I commanded you that you should not eat?" Then the man said, "The woman whom You gave to be with me, she gave me of the tree, and I ate." And the LORD God said to the woman, "What is this you have done?" The woman said, "The serpent deceived me, and I ate." (Gen. 3:9-13)*

Time and again God used the questioning method. First there was a question about the *location* of Adam and Eve, "Where are you?" Then there were questions about the *logic* behind the answer Adam gave, "Who told you that you were naked? Have you eaten from the tree of which I commanded you that you should not eat?" Eve also was the recipient of a question from God, "What is this you have done?"

This is the first time God approached man in grace, and questions were used to draw Adam and Eve into conversation and to expose their sin. This is a valuable lesson for us to learn.

The Lord Jesus frequently used questions in His encounters with individuals. In fact, when people approached Him with a question, rather than answering directly He often turned the question back on them. In the Gospel of Matthew alone, the Lord asked ninety-four questions during evangelistic conversations.[28] Similarly, we find Philip, the only person specifically called an evangelist in scripture,[29] opening his dialogue with the Ethiopian eunuch with a question: "Do you understand what you are reading?" (Acts 8:30). We see a pattern clearly established in scripture that a wise way to approach the sinner is to ask questions.

Some of the many benefits of asking questions are as follows:

[28.] Ibid., p. 62. cited from Paul Weston, 'Evangelicals and Evangelism' in *Not Evangelical Enough*, ed. Iain Taylor, Carlisle: Paternoster, 2003.

[29.] Acts 21:8. I believe that Philip is specifically called an evangelist because he is to be viewed as a pattern evangelist. There are many lessons to be learned from a study of Philip's conversation with the Ethiopian (Acts 8:26-40).

Questions show Consideration

Communicating quickly to someone that you value their input in conversation will set you apart. When you ask someone a sincere question, you show that you value their opinion and are interested in them. You demonstrate respect for them as intelligent, thinking individuals. To show this interest is rare. Most people are so occupied with their own opinions that they have little time to listen to others.

The number one subject people like to talk about is themselves. People love to express their own opinions, and speak of their own thoughts. By asking questions you allow them to do so, and many jump at the opportunity.

Questions make Conversation

A question mark is shaped like a hook and a question acts like a hook, drawing a person into conversation. Answers are normally expected when questions are asked, so, by asking a question, we place enormous pressure on a person to reply. It appears rude not to.

When I commenced door-to-door evangelism, I often offered people a Gospel of John, described what I was giving them, and said, "Thank you" when they took it. Very rarely did any discussion materialise. Little wonder, for I had not encouraged them to engage with me. A very small change of approach made a massive difference. As I offered people the Gospel of John and described what I was giving them, I concluded with a simple question: "Would that be of interest to you?" Suddenly I discovered that people are able, and often willing, to talk about spiritual subjects on their own doorstep.

Questions bring Calmness

People are easily angered when they think they are being "preached at" and angry people make poor listeners. Asking questions removes this problem because people soon realise that they are participants in a conversation. They are not pupils enduring a lecture, or children being told off by a parent, but adults engaged as equals in a conversation of major importance.

When Philip climbed up onto the chariot to converse with the man of Ethiopia, the scroll of Isaiah was unrolled at the passage the man had been reading aloud. Philip sat beside him and, together, they viewed the same scroll and the same subject. Philip began at the same scripture and "preached Jesus to him" (Acts 8:35). He did not approach his target as an adversary but as an assistant. He was a friend, not an enemy. Side by side they examined together a subject of immense significance, and they did so harmoniously.

As a rule, we should make it our goal to maintain calmness in our conversations. As Koukl puts it, if "anyone in the conversation gets mad, then you lose".[30]

Questions give Clarity

Without asking questions and listening to responses, we *cannot* know what a person is thinking. A massive danger

---

[30.] Koukl, *Tactics*, p. 40.

in evangelistic conversations is that participants speak past each other. We think we know what the unbeliever thinks and set out to correct his perceived problems.

Susan was a very pleasant girl in her early twenties. I invited her to an outreach event close to where she lived. When she refused to come, I asked her, "Do you believe in God?" She was very apologetic and said, "I'm sorry, I don't want to tread on your beliefs, but I really don't believe there's a God". After putting her at ease by explaining that I was there to share what I believed with her and was not in the least offended by her expressing what she believed to me, I asked another question: "Why do you not believe in God?" Her reply gave me enlightenment. She said, "Well, I just know that there isn't a man with a long beard who sits in heaven and is with me everywhere I go".

Notice the clarification my question brought. Susan did not believe in God *because she had a false concept of God*. Her atheism was due (at least in part) to a lack of knowledge of God as revealed in scripture. This commenced a long conversation in which I was able to speak of God's attributes and show how these were expressed at Calvary. Susan brought a friend with her to hear the gospel that evening.

Often the greatest effect of asking questions is that the respondent must articulate his own thoughts. This can be a very illuminating experience for him. Many atheists, for example, think that their belief that there is no God is founded upon firm evidence, and is the only logical conclusion possible. They are supported in this self-deception by an abundance of sound bites provided by prominent atheists; however, a few well-placed questions can quickly rock this false confidence. Suddenly, as they try to explain their own belief, they become aware of the shaky foundation upon which they stand.

Questions maintain Consciousness

Have you ever been on the receiving end of a monologue? Did it inspire you or tire you? A well-known myth is that a cobra can hypnotise its prey — it stares and sways while its victim stands transfixed before it, eyes glazed over, unable to make a sound and unable to run. Sound familiar? Sometimes we treat unbelievers like that. We do all the talking while the eyes of our victim glaze over. All they want to do is run.

By contrast, nothing gets the neurons firing in the brain like a question. As every pupil with a zealous teacher knows, being called upon to engage in the conversation gives extra incentive to stay awake and listen.

Questions take Control

Questions are powerful; they put you in control of the conversation. That's right – you are able to determine the course of the conversation. Do you want to talk about the Bible? Ask a question about it. Do you want to talk about God? Just ask the question.

A short while ago I was with a group of friends for coffee. As the initial buzz of talk subsided, one of my friends asked a question about the Bible. The remainder of our time together was spent discussing the topic he introduced. With one question he directed the whole conversation.

How should we ask Questions?

"The wise of heart is called discerning, and sweetness of speech increases persuasiveness ... The heart of the wise makes his speech judicious and adds persuasiveness to his lips. Gracious words are like a honeycomb, sweetness to the soul and health to the body" (Prov. 16:21, 23-24, ESV). Many Proverbs of Solomon are concerned with how to use the tongue to have a positive impact upon others. To be persuasive in our gospel conversations our speech must be wise, pleasant and gracious. By contrast, "A fool's lips walk into a fight, and his mouth invites a beating" (18:6, ESV). Asking questions arrogantly or aggressively, or showing no interest in the responses, will soon bring your conversation to an end.

How can we avoid communicating these wrong attitudes? Before we look at a tone to adopt, let us not forget that "out of the abundance of the heart the mouth speaks" (Matt. 12:34). If we *are* arrogant, uninterested or aggressive in heart it *will* spill over into our conversation. Just as the tongue can be a good index of physical health, so it reveals spiritual health (cf. Jas. 3:2). We must ensure that we are growing spiritually, enjoying the Lord and feeding on His word to represent Him properly before unbelievers.

The enemies of the Saviour admitted that, "no man ever spoke like this Man" (John 7:46). Those who listened to the Lord "marveled at the gracious words which proceeded out of His mouth" (Luke 4:22). The words of a wise man are "gracious" (Eccl. 10:12). We must remember the exhortation:

"Let your speech always be with grace, seasoned with salt, that you may know how you ought to answer each one." (Col. 4:6)

But can this gracious spirit be conveyed in speech and manner? The tone we adopt must show respect, demolish preconceptions, and put a person at ease. Boccardo suggests that we use the same polite and deferential tone that we would use if asking a waitress the way to the washroom in a restaurant.[31] Our manner must communicate the following:

1. Equality. Daniel T. Niles famously said that evangelism is "one beggar telling another beggar where to find bread".[32] Because this is true, we must never communicate an air of superiority. Don't be condescending or proud, for any suggestion of this will be harmful: no one enjoys being treated as a dunce and no one likes a know-all.

2. Empathy. Be an assistant, not an adversary; engage in conversation, not interrogation. While we are at war, it is not against "flesh and blood" (Eph. 6:12). So, be friendly in approach, personally non-judgmental,[33] and sympathetic with people's struggles. Our goal is to cast down "arguments and every high thing that exalts itself against the knowledge of God" (2 Cor. 10:5) and we will only

---

[31.] Boccardo, *Unsilenced*, pp. 47-48.

[32.] Daniel T. Niles, *New York Times*, May 11, 1986.

[33.] We will see later that this does not involve minimising the problem of sin.

be able to do so as we gain the ear of the sinner. People will not listen if we appear uncaring.

3. Engagement. Show a sincere interest in the answers. We are not asking questions simply because it is our duty; we are concerned to know the answers. Be ready to listen carefully. People will be happy to share their thoughts only for as long as you show them this respect; otherwise the conversation will be over before it starts. What you hear will inform the remainder of your discussion.

4. Encouragement. This can be communicated with a smile, and by affirming what is true in the unbeliever's response. Saying "I understand that," or "I agree with you," when a person expresses sorrow at the suffering of children in the world is a proper response. Not everything the unbeliever says will be wrong; give encouragement, and gain their ear, by affirming what is true rather than only attacking what is false.

Simply put, the tone and manner we adopt must communicate no superiority, but a blend of friendliness, interest and sincerity.

What Questions should we ask?

By this point we should be convinced of the biblical authority for, and the practical benefits of, asking questions.

Our conversation must make a connection (with the sinner) and have a direction (to the Saviour). For this to be possible we must learn where the person is and, beginning at that point, lead them step by step towards a full presentation of the gospel of Christ.

Two types of questions are particularly valuable to accomplish these goals. I have called these *Location* questions and *Logic* questions. The first is intended to discover *where* the person is in their thinking on spiritual matters; the second is used to find out *why* the person holds that position.

The Location Question

Genesis 3 provides us with biblical authority to ask this question, for "the LORD God called to Adam and said to him, 'Where are you?'" (Gen. 3:9). Just as Adam was hiding among the trees of the garden, and needed to be located, so people today are hiding behind false ideas about God and their true status before Him. The location question is intended to make clear exactly where a person is in their understanding of God and of salvation.

The location question is some form of "What do you think?" We could ask, for example, "Do you believe in God?" or "Are you sure that you will be in heaven?" or "Are you interested in the Bible?" or "What do you think happens after death?" Each of these questions is asking for an opinion on a relevant spiritual topic. Philip used this approach when he inquired, "Do you understand what you are reading?" (Acts 8:30). The answer will provide essential information about spiritual status and location.

To be as practical as possible, I have included some examples to show how this type of question may work in a cold-calling situation. These examples are not intended as a template to follow. Their objective is to be helpful in illustrating the value of a questioning approach. My questions are in bold; the reply is in standard type.

COLD-CALLING – POSITIVE RESPONSE.

- **Hello, my name is David, I'm just distributing some free Christian literature. Would that be something you're interested in?**

- Yes, thanks.

- **That's great, I really appreciate that. Do you mind me asking, are you sure that you're going to heaven?**

- I hope so.

- **What do you think is required for you to get there?**[34]

- Hmmm, I think if I do the best I can, God will let me in.

Take a moment to analyse what has taken place in the conversation so far. I have given my name, stated my business and asked if the person is interested in Christianity. This is a fair question to ask and the response to it will determine my approach to the remainder of the conversation.

---

[34] A helpful way to formulate this question is: "If you were standing at the gate of heaven and God was to say to you, 'Why should I let you in?', what would you reply?"

On this occasion the answer is positive, which gives me an opportunity to dig deeper. If a person shows interest in spiritual matters, it makes sense to ask, "Are you sure that you're going to heaven?" as this will more clearly reveal their spiritual status. This question also immediately brings home the personal implications of the conversation, and the ultimate issues. The response "I hope so" is a common one. The third question, intended to draw out the person's viewpoint on salvation, is most important. Christian in *The Pilgrim's Progress* asks the same question masterfully: "But what have you to show at that gate ... that may cause that the gate should be opened to you?"[35]

By asking these three location questions, I have learned very quickly that the person is interested in Christianity, hopes to be in heaven, and thinks that good works are the basis upon which a person merits a place there.

Everything in the conversation has flowed easily. I have not preached, yet I have controlled the conversation. The person has given his opinion and I have listened and learned. Each answer leads naturally into the next question. Already a picture has formed of the spiritual location of the person to whom I am speaking.

But what if the response to the first question is less favourable? How should we react if the person is not interested, or is hostile to Christianity? Consider the following example:

[35.] Bunyan, *The Pilgrim's Progress*, p.131.

COLD-CALLING – NEGATIVE RESPONSE.

- **Hello, my name is David. I'm just distributing some free Christian literature. Would that be something you're interested in?**

- No.

- **Oh, I'm sorry to hear that. Do you mind me asking, do you believe in God?**

- No, I'm an atheist.

Once again, analyse the conversation. After introducing myself and stating my business, I have asked the same general question as before, but the answer this time is negative. Where should I go from here?[36] Many would turn away and think there's no point pursuing the matter any further. However, a second question will bring further light. To a negative response I often ask, "Do you believe in God?" because this will more fully reveal their spiritual location.[37]

In this example I have learned that the person is not interested in Christianity and does not believe in the existence of God.

We will revisit these examples later. Simply note that a few well-thought-out location questions can keep you in control, ensure a calm conversation, and reveal the spiritual location of the person to whom you speak.

[36.] I need not become defensive. My question has simply received a sincere answer.

[37.] Sometimes a negative response is clearly hostile. Retreating from the conversation is then the wisest course of action.

I have chosen to illustrate the location questions by their use in cold-calling situations. However, you may be thinking, "I'm not involved in cold-calling evangelism. All I want is some help to talk to my friends". Because the method we are describing is biblically based, the same principles can be applied to every circumstance. Take the following example:

FRIEND/NEIGHBOUR/COLLEAGUE

- **John, you know that I'm a Christian?**
- Yeah.
- **What's your view on that kind of thing?**
- What kind of thing?
- **Christianity.**
- I suppose each to their own.
- **Do you not have any interest in it yourself?**
- Not really.
- **Do you believe there is a God?**
- No, I'm an atheist.

This example relates a workplace conversation. The same principles can be applied, and the conversation runs just as naturally.

Location questions raise a subject in an *inoffensive*

manner and reveal a person's opinion and understanding without seeming preachy. Even if you get no further than gaining insight into the spiritual location of your friend it will enable you to pray more intelligently for them and prepare yourself for future opportunities.

The Logic Question

Once again, Genesis 3 comes to our aid by providing a follow up to the location question. When Adam's reply revealed his fear and nakedness, God spoke again: "Who told you that you were naked?" (Gen. 3:11). God asked Adam how he had reached his conclusion – this is the logic question.

This question is some form of "Why do you think that?" We might ask, "How did you come to that conclusion?" or "What makes you think that?" or "What convinced you of that?" or "On what basis do you believe that?" Each of these questions is asking for a *reason* for the opinion expressed. The answer will reveal the logic underpinning their point of view.

Many believers find this a difficult question to ask. We may feel embarrassed about challenging a person's belief, but this is normal conversation. Suppose you volunteered the information to someone that you were a Christian. Would it not seem normal for that person to ask what convinced you to become a Christian? If they did so, you wouldn't take offence; you would likely jump at the opportunity to tell them. Similarly, when people express their opinion on any subject, you are well within your rights to ask *why* they hold that viewpoint. Once a person makes a claim it is his duty to defend it. As Koukl puts it:

> *The burden of proof is the responsibility someone has to defend or give evidence for his view. Generally, the rule can be summed up this way: Whoever makes the claim bears the burden. The key here is not to allow yourself to be thrust into a defensive position when the other person is making the claim. It's not your duty to prove him wrong. It's his duty to prove his view.*[38]

When this point is appreciated, it makes conversation much easier.

Some years ago, when I attempted to open a conversation about the gospel with someone who responded with "No thanks, I'm an atheist," I was lost for words. What do I say? How do I defend Christianity? Where do I go from here? Very often I just mumbled something like "Sorry to hear that," and scurried away from the conversation with my tail between my legs. Perhaps you also have felt that moment of panic when your attempt to share the gospel has been rebuffed by "I'm an atheist" or some other such claim. I want to assure you that there is no need to become ruffled and defensive. *Always remember that the person who makes the claim bears the burden.* For someone to say, "I'm an atheist" is to make the claim that they have concluded that God does not exist. You have every right to ask how they

---

[38.] Koukl, *Tactics*, p. 59.

reached that conclusion. The next occasion you receive this response just ask the question "What convinced you there is no God?" This is the logic question and it is very effective.

To place the logic question in context, we will expand upon the examples already given.

COLD-CALLING – POSITIVE RESPONSE.

- **Hello, my name is David. I'm just passing in some free Christian literature. Would that be something you're interested in?**

- Yes, thanks.

- **That's great, I really appreciate that. Do you mind me asking, are you sure that you're going to heaven?**

- I hope so.

- **What do you think is required for you to get there?**

- Hmmm, I think if you do the best you can, God will let you in.

- **Okay, what makes you think that?**

- Well, I suppose it seems only fair!

The logic question here is "What makes you think that?" The unbeliever has made clear that she believes entrance into heaven is obtained by those who do the best they can. By asking a question we have discovered that it is her sense of fairness and reasonableness that forms the basis for her belief.

The responses to her belief are many and we will consider her claim in a later chapter.[39] At this stage we just want to note that we have learned much already about this person's belief system. Let us now look at another possible response.

COLD-CALLING – NEGATIVE RESPONSE

- **Hello, my name is David. I'm just passing in some free Christian literature. Would that be something you're interested in?**

- No.

- **Oh, I'm sorry to hear that. Do you mind me asking, do you believe in God?**

- No, I'm an atheist.

- **Okay, I understand. Do you mind telling me what convinced you there was no God?**

- Mmmmm … Science.

- **Right, so you have been convinced by science that there is no God.**

- Yes.

- **Do you mind me asking how science can persuade you of that?**

- Science can explain everything. There's no need for God.

[39.] See chapter 4.

Again, notice the logic questions. The first, "What convinced you there was no God?", is extremely useful when dealing with atheists. Those who claim that God is non-existent usually come across as very sure of their ground. However, when challenged in this way, fear often leaps into their eyes as they realise they must answer for their claim. The response to the question is often an ill-thought-out parroting of some sound bite they have heard or, sometimes, they give no answer at all.

The second logic question is challenging the presuppositions behind the claim that science has convinced a person that there is no God. As will be shown later, the final response is flawed in many ways.[40] At a foundational level, science involves the examination of the natural world. It cannot therefore, by itself, either prove or disprove the existence of the supernatural.

My intent at this stage is just to show that well-placed questions fulfil the principles we have learned from the Lord's conversation with the woman of Samaria. They show respect; they demolish the preconception that Christians are unable and unwilling to listen to views other than their own; they direct the conversation; and they disarm the other party enabling a valuable conversation to take place. The well-known Christian apologist and evangelist Francis Schaeffer used to say that "if he had one hour with someone, he would spend 55 minutes asking them questions, and 5 minutes trying to

---

[40.] See chapter 8

say something that would speak to their situation once he understood a little more about what was going on in their heart and mind."[41] Such dedication to listening is a rare but invaluable discipline for everyday evangelism.

Keeping the Conversation on track

> Then the woman of Samaria said to Him, "How is it that You, being a Jew, ask a drink from me, a Samaritan woman?" For Jews have no dealings with Samaritans. Jesus answered and said to her, "If you knew the gift of God, and who it is who says to you, 'Give Me a drink,' you would have asked Him, and He would have given you living water." The woman said to Him, "Sir, You have nothing to draw with, and the well is deep. Where then do You get that living water? Are You greater than our father Jacob, who gave us the well, and drank from it himself, as well as his sons and his livestock?" Jesus answered and said to her, "Whoever drinks of this water will thirst again, but whoever drinks of the water that I shall give him will never thirst. But the water that I shall give him will become in him a fountain of water springing up into everlasting life." The woman said to Him, "Sir, give me this water, that I may not thirst, nor come here to draw." (John 4:9-15)

There are other aspects in the Lord's approach to the woman which are helpful. He held her attention, and led

---

[41.] Barrs, *Learning Evangelism from Jesus*, p. 69.

her towards the truth of the gospel, in the following ways:

He was Focused

The Lord knew where He was going. When considering the general flow of the conversation we noted that we must make connection and have direction. The Lord was happy to answer genuine challenges; however, to maintain direction in His conversation, He avoided *unnecessary* controversy.

Surprised by the conversation and the request for a drink, the woman asked, "How is it that You, being a Jew, ask a drink from me, a Samaritan woman?" (v. 9). She knew that Jews were not willing to eat and drink from the same containers as Samaritans – this caused her to be taken aback at the Lord's request. By articulating her surprise as she did, the woman introduced the thorny subject of Jewish-Samaritan relationships but, in truth, her question was simply an expression of genuine astonishment. It was not a serious question for which she required a detailed answer. The Lord therefore passed it by, and kept before Him the great priority of the gospel.

Because the Lord had a goal before Him in the conversation, He did not allow Himself to be deflected. Very often people will raise many issues, but we cannot follow every rabbit trail. We must discern which questions or challenges are sincerely raised, and therefore worth spending time discussing.

Imagine you are travelling by train to a chosen destination. As the train thunders along you watch the blur of the passing countryside. Sometimes the train slows and you can take in more of the view. At times it stops at a station and more people get on board while others leave. All of this is no cause for concern, *as long as the train continues on the mainline to the destination*. However, if the train is derailed, or directed onto another track, you would be unhappy, and have every cause for concern. You would never arrive at the intended destination.

Being in a gospel conversation is much like being on a train journey. Sometimes it is beneficial to slow down and consider in greater detail some aspect of the journey. Occasionally we should stop to take on board new information and let it settle. However, we should not allow ourselves to be deflected from the gospel mainline or derailed by a thorny subject. The direction must be maintained so that the destination can be reached.

Learn to keep the big thing the big thing. While you may end up chatting about subjects which you can't avoid (such as same-sex marriage and abortion), always remember that the person with whom you converse is a lost soul and needs the Saviour. Remember to speak of Christ as soon as it is appropriate to do so. If you are not able in this conversation, then, perhaps, in the next one.

He was Passionate

Positivity can be infectious. The Lord's communication of the gospel was enthusiastic and passionate. "If you knew the gift of God, and who it is who says to you, 'Give Me a drink,' you would have asked Him, and He would have given you living water." (v. 10). He showed complete confidence in the message by stating that, if she would properly evaluate what was being offered, she would certainly ask for it. Evidently the Lord's words were intended to whet her appetite and appeal to her curiosity. If she but knew the gift and the Giver, she would most certainly request and receive the blessing.

The Christian gospel is a positive message and there is therefore an earnestness and enthusiasm which befits its communication to others. Sin is serious and hell is dreadful – this should make us earnest. The gospel which promises deliverance from both sin and hell should make us enthusiastic. Meditation on the blessings of the gospel and the beauties of the Saviour will enable us to communicate positively and persuasively. "You cannot expect others to become excited ... unless you are capable of genuinely reflected emotion".[42]

The story is often told of a preacher and an actor. Many people listened to the preacher proclaiming the gospel and were unmoved. Later, the same people watching the actor's performance in a theatre were moved to tears. Noticing this, the preacher asked the actor, "Why do people remain unaffected when I speak of eternal realities, while, when you are dealing in fiction, many are deeply affected?" The actor replied, "You speak of facts as if they were fiction, but I speak of fiction as if it were fact." When dealing with facts of eternal consequence to sinners, your manner must properly represent your message.

---

[42] Joe Carter and John Coleman, *How To Argue Like Jesus: Learning Persuasion From History's Greatest Communicator*, Crossway, 2009, p. 30.

While we cannot forget the seriousness of sin and the awfulness of hell, the gospel message is not merely the announcement of an escape route from hell fire. A sinner who believes in Christ is reconciled to the God who made him, released from the dominion of sin, and reserved for eternal glory. Do not undersell the gospel. Salvation should not be communicated as a necessary evil but as the greatest blessing anyone could ever have. It is truly a wonderful thing to be saved.

The gospel can therefore be shared with a smile on your face and with sincere gratitude in your heart. Speak of your relationship with the Lord as if He means something to you. Bring in your own experience if it serves the purpose of conveying the wonder of salvation. In Mark 5, the Lord sent the man who had once been demon-possessed back to his friends and family with the instruction to "tell them what great things the Lord has done for you, and how He has had compassion on you" (Mark 5:19).

Once, in a very long conversation with an atheist, I had covered such topics as the evidence for God's existence, the reliability of the Bible, the evidence for the resurrection of Christ, and more. While she listened well and was fair in her attitude to what I said, she remained unimpressed and unaffected. Just before I left her, I told her that I got saved when I was twenty-one years old. I shared with her how the Lord had changed my life, giving me freedom from the burden of guilt and giving purpose to my existence. I told of my satisfaction with what I had received and how the Lord had given me power to live a different kind of life. Immediately her attitude was transformed: she was interested, even eager, to hear more of what salvation meant.

A salesperson not only presents what his product *is* but what it *does*. On a bottle of hair-restoring tablets the ingredients will be somewhere in small print. However, the words "hair restoring" will be emblazoned all over the packaging. To the consumer this is the important point. For many people the final confirmation of the gospel's value is: "Does it work?" and, thank God, it does. We can therefore enthusiastically recommend it, as the Lord did here.

He was Understanding
Conversation is two-way communication and, as the Lord continued His conversation with the woman, she raised a challenge. His claim to give "living water" was questioned: "The woman said to Him, "Sir, You have nothing to draw with, and the well is deep. Where then do You get that living water? Are You greater than our father Jacob, who gave us the well, and drank from it himself, as well as his sons and his livestock?" (4:11-12).

The Lord did not interrupt her, but allowed her to speak. He did not speak over her or dismiss her objection. He listened to her challenge and responded to it. He was sufficiently relaxed to allow her to contribute freely, so that the conversation unfolded naturally. Her contribution, while presented as a challenge, revealed that her understanding of both gift and Giver were incorrect. She thought she was still engaged only at a natural level in a conversation that concerned merely physical needs.

From a human standpoint, if the Lord had not allowed her to speak, her misunderstanding would not have been revealed and could not have been rectified.[43] We can learn to view interruptions as opportunities to learn more, making us better informed to lead a person towards the truth. Refusal to allow a person to take part freely in a conversation is a sure way to end it.

He was Relevant

The Lord also maintained her interest by His use of everyday analogies. This is characteristic of many of the conversations He engaged in. Physical objects and everyday matters were often employed to illustrate spiritual realities.

On this occasion, the conversation took place at a well with a woman who had come with her water pot to get water. In keeping with this, the Lord invested His conversation with subjects such as water, drinking, thirst, and a well. A quick read through the Gospel narratives will show that He was not limited to this analogy. In John 3 He used an Old Testament story with Nicodemus, a man familiar with the Jewish scriptures (vv. 14-15). In John 10, He used the analogy of shepherding to illustrate many salvation truths.

Although we live in a different culture and time to the Lord Jesus, the principle of illustrating unfamiliar truth by means of everyday objects and events is still important.

[43.] Of course, the Lord knew every detail of her thoughts before she expressed them. However, *we* do not know people's thoughts before they speak and so the lesson is pertinent.

People quickly relate to something that they know, and can grasp the spiritual significance more easily.

I remember speaking to Amy, a girl who stated that she was not religious but "spiritual". I asked her what she meant by that and she said that she just felt she was "connected". She was, in her view, in touch with the supernatural and with God, simply because she felt so. I told her how I had once purchased a laptop and a projector. Having brought them home, I found they were incompatible. Before they could work together, I needed to buy a connection which made the projector compatible with the laptop. Quoting Paul's words to Timothy, "there is one God and one Mediator between God and men, the Man Christ Jesus, who gave Himself a ransom for all ... " (1 Tim. 2:5-6), I explained that we are incompatible with God because of our sin, and that there is only one, "the Man Christ Jesus", who can remove the problem and truly connect us with God. She listened intently and seemed to understand my point.

You may think that the illustration I used was not one you would have employed. That's fine; just find one you consider more appropriate. Perhaps you think that you could not come up with a suitable analogy on the spur of the moment. Here is the secret – I didn't think of it on the spur of the moment either. I had prepared myself earlier with suitable illustrations of a mediator, and was therefore ready when the occasion arose.

To some people it is very natural to use simple word-illustrations to clarify a point. To others it is less so. However, like questioning, it is a skill that can be learned and will quickly become a habit. Suppose you had an exam for which to prepare and had to think up analogies to explain some difficult concepts — when the time came you would be prepared. The challenge is to prepare simple illustrations of gospel concepts now, based on everyday life, so that you are ready when opportunity knocks.

It didn't work!

Having a biblical approach to conversing with unbelievers does not guarantee a positive response. A brief consideration of the ministry of the Lord Jesus will confirm this. Do not be too discouraged if your attempts to share the gospel are rebuffed. Many people are determined, for whatever reason, to avoid the subject. In these circumstances, rather than force the issue, you are much better to turn to God in prayer. God desires the salvation of all (cf. 1 Tim. 2:1-6) and He can be trusted to bring circumstances to bear upon individuals to remind them of their need.

Emma works at my local barber's shop. One day, as she was cutting my hair, I tried to have a conversation on spiritual matters. She answered every question with, "I wouldn't know". She was shutting down the conversation and I gave up, feeling defeated. However, because I didn't force the issue (and because I gave her a tip) we parted on good terms. Afterwards, I put her on the prayer list and began to pray for her. A year later she was cutting my hair again and asked me what I had planned for the evening. When I said I was going to preach the gospel, and tentatively asked for her opinion, she unexpectedly replied, "I'd love to know God." Suddenly I had an excellent opportunity to share the gospel with the same person who had shut me up twelve months earlier. During the conversation I found out that she had been brought up as a Mormon, and her experience with religion had not been positive. Likely this was why she refused to converse the first time. It is wise to leave such people with God, and pray for them; you may be surprised how their attitude changes.

Chapter 3

BRINGING CONVICTION

The title of this chapter is likely to be challenged. Can we bring conviction? Is that not the work of the Holy Spirit? Of course it is. There is no doubt that bringing conviction is beyond our ability – it is God's work. However, the Bible clearly teaches that the Spirit of God uses *means* to convict people. Notice how the Lord brought conviction in the case of the woman of Samaria.

Why should I bring Conviction?

Jack attended a gospel meeting and heard the truth "if the Son makes you free, you shall be free indeed" (John 8:36). The second sermon he heard was also on the subject of freedom, based on the text, "In Him we have redemption through His blood, the forgiveness of sins, according to the riches of His grace" (Eph. 1:7). Jack was deeply impressed; this was music to his ears because it promised that his life could be changed; he could be liberated from his alcoholism. He could have a normal life and perhaps be reunited with his family. No longer need he remain a social outcast. Jack was affected, and understandably so. A short time later, a Christian visited Jack and led him in a prayer of commitment to Christ. Jack was more than willing to be led, considering what was being offered.

This all sounds great, but there is an essential missing ingredient – Jack never faced up to the reality of his sin. He considered himself a *sufferer*, not a *sinner*. He felt dissatisfied with life, but he never thought himself disobedient to God. From his perspective, he was the victim of circumstances, not the perpetrator of crimes against God. So he welcomed the gospel merely as the answer to his physical, temporal, emotional, and relational needs. He was quick to profess faith in Christ, but showed no fruit whatsoever. He remains an alcoholic to this day.

Returning to the Lord's conversation with the woman of Samaria we can see that, in the early stages of the discussion, the Lord made no mention of sin. He spoke of a blessing from God which is free: "the gift of God" (John 4:10), and which brings satisfaction: "whoever drinks of the water that I shall give him will never thirst" (v. 14). He also introduced the subject of "everlasting life" (v. 14). However, while the Lord whetted her appetite, her understanding of what was on offer remained incorrect or, at best, incomplete.

The gift sounded wonderful, but the woman still thought of it merely as a means of alleviating her natural desires and wants. She replied, "Sir, give me this water, that

I may not thirst, nor come here to draw" (v. 15). She was still thinking of *physical* water because she was only concerned with her physical need. For her to properly evaluate the *spiritual* blessing being offered to her, her spiritual need must be exposed. In order to achieve this, her conscience must be stirred. This the Lord sets out to do. In personal evangelism, this is essential.

How can I bring Conviction?

Jesus said to her, "Go, call your husband, and come here." The woman answered and said, "I have no husband." Jesus said to her, "You have well said, 'I have no husband,' for you have had five husbands, and the one whom you now have is not your husband; in that you spoke truly." The woman said to Him, "Sir, I perceive that You are a prophet." (vv. 16-19)

The Lord made a simple request and in so doing introduced the problem of her personal sin. There are three points to note here:

1. His Target
When the Lord said, "Go, call your husband, and come here" (v. 16) He was not making a random request; His goal was to touch her conscience. Being the Son of God, He knew every detail of her past and His words were deliberately chosen to remind her of sin. His target was her conscience.

2. His Method

How did the Lord reach His target? He said, "Go, call your husband, and come here" (v. 16). This immediately highlighted the woman's relationship with the man with whom she currently lived. It reminded her of life choices which she knew to be sinful. The Lord's approach to the issue was not to speak generally of sin as an abstract idea, but to remind her of *her* sin – a concrete reality in her life. This woman had transgressed moral boundaries, broken divine laws, and committed sins. The memory of her own sinful choices became the highway to her conscience.

While the Lord brought to the woman's attention her sin, He did so without direct accusation. To accuse her would have raised her defences and might have caused her to deny wrongdoing – such is the pride of the human heart. The Lord chose a more *indirect* approach to *lead her to acknowledge the problem first.*

3. His Result

Her response was, "I have no husband" (v. 17). There have been many suggestions as to what the woman intended by this answer. Some have suggested that it was a lie. However, the Lord affirms just the opposite: "You have well said, 'I have no husband,' for you have had five husbands, and the one whom you now have is not your husband; in that you spoke truly" (vv. 17-18).

When she said, "I have no husband," she was making an admission of her present marital status – that much is obvious. She did not immediately volunteer information about her past, but she would be drawn into the admission of her past when the Lord unfolded it to her. After the Lord revealed her history, she confirmed the accuracy of His account with the words, "Sir, I perceive that You are a prophet" (v. 19). This was a tacit admission that the Lord's assessment of her past life and present circumstances was correct. It was a confession, and this is undoubtedly the crisis of the conversation. From this point onwards, her contribution to the conversation takes on a spiritual dimension. She has previously considered Him a Jew (v. 9) and spoken about water (vv. 11, 12, 15), now she calls Him a prophet (v. 19) and speaks about worship (v. 20).

By taking aim at her conscience and reminding her of past sin the Lord paved the way for spiritual conversation.

How can we learn from His approach? We must likewise aim for the conscience, deal in concrete moral realities, and encourage the agreement of the sinner with the divine assessment of their sins.

1. Our Target

While we may not know the past sins of any with whom we converse, yet we do know that everyone *has* a shameful past. Conscience is our ally. While not everyone has sinned in the same way or to the same degree, everyone has sinned in some way and to some degree. Knowing this we must, as the Lord did, set out to bring this to their remembrance.

2. Our Method

The Lord spoke of *specific* sin, and we must learn to do the same. Often conviction is not brought about through a general statement of man's sinfulness, but by personal awareness of specific sin. David, after the numbering of the people, said, "I have sinned greatly in what I have done" (2 Sam. 24:10). It is this response which we must seek to bring about (by the Spirit's power) in those with whom we converse. We must make people consider their personal sin against God.

It is not always wise or helpful to be confrontational in this matter. There is a time for the shock tactic of direct accusation, but this is not the normal method. If possible, we should lead a person to acknowledge their own guilt rather than directly accusing them. I do not mean that we should tell them to merely repeat words of confession after us, but that we should allow the conviction of sin to produce the fruit of confession. It is much more effective when they admit their own guilt than when you assert it.

To re-emphasise this, we can refer back to the garden of Eden. Consider how the first evangelist, God, sought to bring the sinful couple to acknowledge their guilt before Him. To Adam He said, "Have you eaten from the tree of which I commanded you that you should not eat?" (Gen. 3:11), and to Eve He said, "What is this you have done?" (v. 13). Put simply, He aimed for the conscience, dealt in specifics, and encouraged the guilty couple to own up to their own sin.

3. Our Result
Our goal is that the sinner agrees with God about his sin. Confession of sin (which involves genuine admission

of personal guilt) is the foundation of true repentance. Repentance, properly understood, is a change of mind by which the sinner aligns himself with what God says. God says that, because of crimes committed against Him, the sinner is guilty before Him. The sinner's first step towards salvation is to acknowledge that God's assessment of him is accurate.

What brings Conviction?

Is there a means of bringing conviction? I think there is. Does its use agree with the principles we have just drawn from the Lord's conversation with the woman of Samaria, and with the conversation in Eden? I believe it does. The means is biblical, and its use is generally applicable, easily understood, and very practical.

A Biblical Means

The epistle to the Romans provides the fullest exposition of the way of salvation in all of scripture. As Paul wraps up the first major section of the epistle (in which he has shown the guilt of man), he writes: "By the deeds of the law no flesh will be justified in His sight, for by the law is the knowledge of sin" (Rom. 3:20). God's law gives awareness of sin. As Luther put it, its purpose is "not to justify, but to terrify".[44] Paul shows how this worked in his experience: "I would not have known sin except through the law. For I would not have known covetousness unless the law had

---

[44.] Luther, cited in Precept Austin,
http://www.preceptaustin.org/romans_520-21.

said, '*You shall not covet.*'" (7:7). Sin was shown to be sinful, and known to be sinful, by the law.

To know that we have fallen short, there must be a standard to measure ourselves against. To know that we have strayed from a path, there must be a clearly-marked path to follow. To perceive something to be crooked, we must have some idea of what is meant by straight. Thankfully God has, in the law, provided His standard, His path, and His straight-edge.

In 1 Timothy 1 Paul taught that "the law is good if one uses it lawfully" (v. 8). Used in accordance with its intended purpose, the law is exceedingly beneficial in evangelism. It cannot *erase* sin, but it can *expose* sin by revealing the proper standard against which human conduct is measured.

Without an objective standard, the tendency within the human heart is to compare one's self with others, or to make up a standard of morality which agrees with what we do rather than challenges or condemns it. The law of God, however, condemns our activity because it is a divinely provided revelation of God's glory.

The law is not the answer to our problem; it was never intended to be that. It simply makes us aware of the problem. In this way, the law has been compared to a mirror. When someone looks in the mirror, he sees what he looks like. If he has dirt on his face, the mirror will expose it. However, the mirror cannot remove it; water and soap are required for that.

While we have a sound doctrinal basis for using the law in evangelism, we might wonder if any practical examples can be found in scripture. Returning to the garden of Eden we see the method God used to bring before Adam his sin. He said: "Have you eaten from the tree of which I commanded you that you should not eat?" (Gen. 3:11), and to Eve He said, "What is this you have done?" (v. 13). He reminded Adam of the law He had set, and He asked Adam whether his conduct was in keeping with the commandment given. This was intended to bring conviction: to cause the first man to see that his action was no mere misstep or weakness. What Adam had done was to rebel against God's authority by transgressing His law.

The Lord Jesus used the law on a number of occasions with this same purpose in view. In Luke 10, we read:

> *And behold, a certain lawyer stood up and tested Him, saying, "Teacher, what shall I do to inherit eternal life?" He said to him, "What is written in the law? What is your reading of it?" So he answered and said, "'You shall love the Lord your God with all your heart, with all your soul, with all your strength, and with all your mind,' and 'your neighbor as yourself.'" And He said to him, "You have answered rightly; do this and you will live." But he, wanting to justify himself, said to Jesus, "And who is my neighbor?" (vv. 25-29)*

This is the context in which the Lord told the well-known story of the good Samaritan. Notice how the conversation unfolded. An expert in the Old Testament asked what was required to inherit eternal life. Luke reveals to his readers that the man was not sincere in his question;

as a recognised expert, he was bursting to express his own knowledge.

The Lord gives him the floor. Turning the question back on him, He says, "What is written in the law? What is your reading of it?" Here was the opportunity the lawyer wanted; the answer is on the tip of his tongue and he quickly responds by quoting from the Old Testament concerning man's responsibility to love God with all of his being and his neighbour as himself. The Lord did not argue with the lawyer's answer; rather, He affirmed it: "do this and you will live."

How would you have answered the challenge? Perhaps you would have been at pains to disagree with the lawyer, and to stress that eternal life is the "gift of God" (Rom. 6:23). However, the Lord Jesus took the lawyer up on his own ground because *what the lawyer said was correct.* To obtain eternal life based on our own actions we *must* love God with all of our being, and love our neighbours as ourselves. This is the spine of Old Testament law; on these two commandments "hang all the Law and the Prophets" (Matt. 22:40). It is necessary then to carefully assess what keeping God's law would require.

It is vital to understand that only *complete* and *continual* obedience could be accepted. To say that you have kept any law partially or sporadically is to admit that you have broken it, and therefore deserve to pay the penalty. Paul confirms this in Galatians 3: "For all who rely on works of the law are under a curse; for it is written, 'Cursed be everyone who does not abide by all things written in the

Book of the Law, and do them.'" (v. 10, ESV). The only way to be declared right before God on the basis of law-keeping is to obey all of God's commandments all of the time.

Loving God with all the heart, soul, mind, and strength is a standard far above the reality of fallen human experience in this world. It demands that every decision taken is made out of devotion to God, in obedience to His will, and with a single eye for His glory. It requires wholehearted delight in all that God is and does. It demands that every ounce of physical energy be expended joyfully in constant, devoted, obedient, and sacrificial service toward God. It requires that the intellect be willingly submitted to God's word, exercised in gaining knowledge of God and His ways, and utilised to further God's purpose in the world. It is important to see that this is not merely a standard toward which we should aim; it is a law which we must always have kept. Not one moment of half-hearted love toward God is permitted if we are to gain eternal life by works.

Of course, this Old Testament scholar knew he had never lived like this, and we know that we haven't either. The unbeliever has never reached this standard; every conscious moment of his life has been lived in transgression of God's law.[45]

The lawyer also added that we must love our neighbours as ourselves. To love someone as you love yourself is to never prioritise yourself over them; it is to always treat

---

[45.] An unsaved person may have obeyed individual commands of the law. For example, a happily married man may never have committed adultery. However, an unbeliever has never, at any time, loved God with all of his being.

them as you would love to be treated. I remember hearing this illustrated in the following way:

Suppose you live in a small town and take a walk one evening into the countryside. As you reach the edge of town a fire engine races past you in the opposite direction, sirens blaring. You wonder if you have left the oven on at home and a fire has started. Gazing back over the town you can see the orange flames in the general area where you live. Dismayed, you begin to rush back towards your home. As you get nearer, you can see that the fire is in the very street where you live; your pace quickens. With heart pounding, you turn into your street … What a relief! It's not *your* house on fire, it's your *neighbour's*.

This is a very natural response; which of us would not have acted like this? However, when assessed by the law of God, we can see clearly that this is not loving our neighbour as ourselves; this is breaking God's law.

Whether it be love for God or love for neighbours, honesty demands that we admit that we are law-breakers. We are criminals standing before a righteous judge awaiting the execution of His sentence.

But someone might say: "Why doesn't God lower His standard? If He wants us to be in heaven, why not make the law more lenient?" The answer to this is that it is *impossible* for God to do so. We may argue that it is inevitable that we will break God's law because of what we are; by the same logic we must see that it is impossible for Him to lower the standard because of who He is. We don't reach it because we are sinners; He can't lower it because He is righteous.

God cannot demand less than perfection from man. His laws are not arbitrary contrivances – they are reflections of His own perfect character. The person who has loved God and his fellow man as God requires has never sinned, and God can demand nothing less than sinless perfection. To reduce this demand would show simply that holiness and righteousness are not very important to God.

The Lord Jesus agreed with what the lawyer *said*, but He knew well that this was not what the lawyer *did*. He then took the lawyer further than he wanted to go by saying, "*do this and you will live*" (Luke 10:28, emphasis added). Rather than being pleased at Jesus' agreement with his answer, the conscience of the lawyer was awakened; his next words were said in an attempt to "justify himself" (v. 29).

The law had done its work. And, while the lawyer would try to wriggle away from its convicting power, the Lord would not let him off the hook easily. When asked, "And who is my neighbor?", the Saviour told the parable of the good Samaritan. This showed the lawyer's responsibility to love his most bitter enemies! This would serve to drive home with even greater force his guilt.

When the Lord used the law, his purpose was not the immediate *conversion* of the lawyer, but his *conviction*. "Such people need … to hear the Law clearly first and to be told to go and keep that Law, so that they might discover that they cannot keep it and come back humbled and prepared to hear the good news of the Gospel of forgiveness".[46] Jesus

---

[46.] Jerram Barrs, *The Heart of Evangelism*, InterVarsity Press, 2001, p.226.

did not give the man a direct answer to his need; He did, however, make him aware of his need. This is an important part of evangelism.

These are not the only occasions in scripture when God's law is applied practically to make a person conscious of their sin against God.[47] To use the law in this way is certainly biblical.

A Universal Means

The use of the law to bring conviction is not only biblical but universal in its application. How can this be? Surely only those who know the law and accept it as authoritative can be convicted by it?

People who have never heard the law are the subject of Romans 2. Paul confirms that those who do not have an external written law, still have the "work of the law written in their hearts" (v. 15). They possess a moral consciousness, a divinely implanted awareness of right and wrong,

> ... for when Gentiles, who do not have the law, by nature do the things in the law, these, although not having the law, are a law to themselves, who show the work of the law written in their hearts, their conscience also bearing witness, and between themselves their thoughts accusing or else excusing them. (vv. 14-15)

In the context, Paul shows that people who do not have the external written law of God will still be held accountable

---

[47.] e.g. the rich young ruler (Luke 18:18-23). Romans chapter 2, which reveals principles of God's righteous judgment, also has very interesting insight; see vv. 6-10.

for their actions. He gives three lines of evidence to confirm that moral awareness exists altogether apart from a written code of commandments:

1. When a person does what is right, his **Conduct** confirms his moral awareness

When "Gentiles, who do not have the law, by nature do the things in the law, these, although not having the law, are a law to themselves" (v. 14). This could be illustrated as follows: Suppose a person is in trouble and knows that a lie would get him out of trouble, yet he decides to tell the truth anyway. Why would he tell the truth? If there is no merely pragmatic reason, then it is because he knows that it is *right* to tell the truth and *wrong* to tell a lie.

Take a more extreme example. Two men are shipwrecked and stranded together on a desert island with a very small supply of food. Because there are two of them the food supply dwindles very quickly. However, each one hesitates to kill the other. It would make perfect sense to do so from a purely pragmatic point of view. They will never be found out; there is no law on their island demanding they do not kill each other. Why do they not do so? They do not kill each other because they know it would be wrong for them to do so.

Every time a person does what is good for no other reason than that he perceives it to be good, he is proving the "work of the law" written on his heart.

2. When a person does what is wrong, his Conscience confirms his moral awareness

Paul continues, "their conscience also bearing witness" (v. 15). Some may respond to our previous point by saying that people do not always do good. This is obviously true. In most instances, people would just tell the lie; and in circumstances such as I have described, some would just kill their companion on a desert island.

While this is correct, it is also true that upon telling the lie, or committing the murder, something else begins to happen. The conscience of the person is aroused to give further evidence of moral culpability. There is an accusing voice within which rises up and screams — "that was wrong," "you shouldn't have done that," "that was a lie," "that was murder." Therefore, whether we do good, or do evil, there is evidence that we are moral agents, making choices based on moral awareness.

3. When one person judges another, his Criticism confirms his moral awareness

The final proof of moral awareness is stated, "and between themselves their thoughts accusing or else excusing them" (v. 15). On 11th September 2001, the world reeled in shock from the attack on the Twin Towers in New York. Passenger jets were flown into the towers, causing death and destruction on a massive scale. On the front page of newspapers, on television reports, in conversation in workplaces, and in family discussions, many words were used to describe the attacks and the attackers. The attackers were evil, wicked, cruel; the actions shameful, vile, wrong.

All those who made statements of condemnation confirmed the "work of the law written in their hearts". When we judge another person's actions to be right or wrong, we show that there is a standard of morality by which we make our assessment. That standard is the moral law.

Every person has some awareness of right and wrong, good and evil. Remember this as you evangelise. You have an ally within the person you are trying to reach. While many may deny this, yet they do so against what they know to be true. A person may deny that telling lies is wrong, however, when their spouse lies to them, they are righteously indignant. Because of this, the use of the law is relevant to all. Very often, even in conversation with those who profess to be atheists, much argument can be bypassed by going directly to the standards of God's law and applying them.

A Logical Means

The law makes a logical bridge between a person's wrongdoing and their punishment. Many people view their sins merely as imperfections and weaknesses, but not as crimes. Because of this they cannot understand that they deserve punishment. Some fear hell, but they do not believe that they deserve to be there.

How can people be convinced that sin deserves

punishment, and that hell is righteous judgment? It is at this point that the law comes into its own. People know how law works; they understand that there is a difference between law and advice. Advice is something we can take or leave. While it often would be better that we follow advice, there is no certain penalty for refusing to do so. Law is different, for there is a penalty attached to each crime committed. As is often said: if we do the crime, we must do the time. The process of law can be summarised as follows:

1. There is a *law*.

2. To break it is to commit a *crime*.

3. To commit a crime is to be *guilty*.

4. To be guilty is to deserve *punishment*.

Society is founded upon this, and people do not often argue against the justice of such a process. Evangelistically, this can be applied in this way:

1. There is the *law of God*.

2. To break it is to commit a *crime against God*.

3. To commit a crime against God is to be *guilty before God*.

4. To be guilty before God is to deserve *punishment from God*.

Notice how this provides the bridge between our sins and God's punishment. *The law shows sin to be sinful and judgment to be just.* By the help of God we must show people that they are not only on the way to hell, but that their sins are *deserving* of that judgment. God is perfectly righteous in their condemnation. We must seek to convince them of this in order to properly represent the God of the Bible. God's law makes a logical bridge between a person's sins and God's judgment.

A Practical Means

While the use of the law to bring conviction is a biblical, universal, and logical approach, you may be wondering what this looks like in everyday evangelism. How is the law applied practically in order to bring conviction? Here is a sample conversation:

PRACTICAL USE OF THE LAW[48]

- **Are you sure of being in heaven?**

- I hope so!

- **How do you think that a person gets there?**

- By being good. Doing the best you can.

- **Would you say that you are a good person?**

- Yes.

- **Have you ever heard of the Ten Commandments?**

- Yes.

---

[48] I was first introduced to this method in Ray Comfort, *The Way of the Master: How to share your faith simply, effectively, biblically … the way Jesus did*, Bridge-Logos, 2006.

- **You understand that they are God's law? What that means is, if you break them you are guilty.**

- Yes.

- **Well, one of them says, "You shalt not bear false witness." You shouldn't tell lies. Have you ever done that?**

- Of course I have; everyone has.

- **So if you were to stand before God and be judged by that law, would you be innocent or guilty?**

- Guilty! [At this point sometimes the person looks stunned.]

- **Okay, we'll take another one. The Law says that you should not take God's name in vain. You shouldn't use His name in a careless way – as a swear word, for example. Have you ever done that?**

- Sometimes.

- **So if you were to stand before God and be judged by that law, would you be innocent or guilty?**

- Guilty!

- **Okay, so imagine you are in court and you have been found guilty of a crime, what does the judge do next?**

- Punishes you, sends you to prison.

- **Yes, and the Bible says God punishes us if we are guilty. Does that concern you?**

- Well, yes, I suppose it does.

While you may be thinking that this conversation is idealised, I have had many such conversations. There is usually more to them than what has been recorded but this gives the bare bones of those encounters.

This dialogue need not be a template for every discussion – it is not intended to be. It is best, if possible, to tailor your use of the law to the immediate need. It sometimes becomes clear which commandment is best to focus upon. Recently I had a chat with a middle-aged man called Sam. During the discussion Sam pointed out the needs of the homeless and showed moral outrage at the lack of love in society: "People should all love one another and not be so selfish!" A few minutes later, when the opportunity arose to speak of the law, I used his own words to challenge his conscience.[49] The conversation went like this:

- **You mentioned that there was a lack of love in society, and you really seemed to care a lot about that; am I right?**

- Yes I do care.

- **Well, God cares a lot about it too. In fact, His law demands that we love our neighbour as we love ourselves. What do you think of that?**

[49.] This was the technique used by Nathan when he challenged King David about his sin with Bathsheba (2 Sam. 12:1-14).

- It makes sense – if we all truly loved each other the troubles in the world would soon disappear.

- **It would certainly make a big difference to society! If we loved like that none of us would ever act selfishly at any time. The problem is that I certainly haven't been unselfish all the time – have you?**

- Well, not all the time – no one's perfect.

- **I know. That's the problem isn't it? This is God's law. If you haven't kept it then that means you've broken it. Put it like this: If you were to stand before God and be judged by the law: "Love your neighbour as yourself," would you be innocent or guilty?**

- I suppose I would be guilty.

- **And, if you are guilty, that means you deserve to be punished. There's a penalty for breaking God's law. Does that concern you?**

- Maybe, a little, but ...

Often, by employing this method, I have witnessed a change in the attitude of the person with whom I am in conversation. The levity and unconcern is removed, and a troubled look appears. Faces have changed colour as people suddenly realize that they stand guilty before God and deserve His punishment.

In the Lord's conversation with the woman at the well, we noted three features of the method the Lord used to bring conviction: He aimed for the conscience, dealt with specific sins, and led her to confess her problem. Now, look again at the use of the law above. Does this incorporate these three features? We are aiming for the conscience, we are also dealing with specific sins, and we are encouraging them to admit their own guilt.

While those who confess their guilt in conversation are often not truly convicted of their guilt before God, yet a line has been crossed. They have been confronted with the righteousness and reasonableness of punishment and it should become hard for them to "kick against the goads" (Acts 9:5). The law has made their sin appear more than a character fault or a mistake – it has shown their sin to be a crime against God which righteously deserves His judgment. It has shown sin to be sinful and judgment to be just.

The Criminal's Defence

Not everyone sits silent in the dock accepting God's verdict. Some people will refuse to accept that they are guilty, even with such a clear case against them. How can we respond if they refuse to acknowledge their guilt?

There are several pleas made in defence, whether to claim innocence or to mitigate guilt. However, each defence offered by the criminal in God's court would be dismissed if it were presented as a defence in a law court in this world. I have given a few examples below:

TIME OF THE CRIME

- **Would you be innocent or guilty?**

- Innocent.

- **Why do you think that?**

- Well, I may have told some lies years ago when I was a child, but I never tell them now.

- **Okay. Let's suppose that's true. Imagine you were in court for a murder you committed twenty years ago. Would the judge find you not guilty because you didn't commit the crime today?**

- No, I suppose not.

- **Exactly, so would you be innocent or guilty?**

- Guilty.

Notice the foolishness of the defence. Time does not remove crime.

CHARITABLE CRIMINAL

- **Would you be innocent or guilty?**

- Innocent.

- **Why do you think that?**

- God would consider the good things I have done and find me not guilty.

- Okay. Imagine you were in court for beating up an old lady and you said to the judge: "Wait, I helped another old lady across the road!" Would the judge find you not guilty?

- No.

- Exactly, because the reason you are guilty has nothing to do with the good you've done, it is all to do with the bad you've done. So would you be innocent or guilty?

- Guilty.

Crimes are not nullified by charitable works.

CRIME COMPARISON

- Would you be innocent or guilty?

- Innocent.

- Why do you think that?

- Well, I haven't killed anyone. There are people who are much worse than I am.

- I'm sure that's true, but imagine you were in court for a burglary. You say to the judge, "I haven't murdered anyone." The judge would say, "Glad to hear it, but that has no relevance to this case. You're charged with burglary and you have done that." Would you be found guilty or not guilty?

- Guilty.

- **Exactly, and God is not going to charge you with anything you haven't done, only with what you *have* done. So, to get back to the point, would you be innocent or guilty before God?**

- Guilty.

In court your actions are not compared with the actions of others. They are assessed by the demands of the law.

Severe Sentencing

Some may object that it would be unfair of God to punish anyone in hell. However, when the law is used to show a person their guilt before God, the idea of punishment naturally follows, and often when hell is mentioned no challenge is raised. There are, however, some challenges which do arise and these concern the severity of the punishment, either because the suffering in hell seems extreme or because it is eternal.

Below are a few approaches to dealing with the objections which might be raised. At this stage, we are not considering any in-depth defence of God's right to send sinners to eternal conscious punishment,[50] we are simply using the whole concept of law and justice to remove the perceived problem as quickly as possible.

[50.] For this, read Paul McCauley, *He that Believeth Not: The Errors of Universalism and Annihilationism Explored*, John Ritchie Ltd, 2016.

EXTREME PUNISHMENT

- **Would you be innocent or guilty?**

- Technically, I would be guilty, but God wouldn't send me to hell.

- **Why do you think that?**

- Well, I know I've sinned, but there is no way I should be in hell. My sin doesn't deserve hell fire.

- **Okay, suppose a criminal was in court. He's done murder. He doesn't think he should go to prison. Should he be the one to decide?**

- No, of course not.

- **As a matter of fact, the last person who should decide his sentence is the criminal; would you not agree? Who will decide what his sentence is?**

- The judge.

- **That's right. The judge knows the law and the proper penalty for the crime. In our case, God is the judge and He has decided the sentence. The punishment fits the crime in His eyes.**

ETERNAL PUNISHMENT

- **Would you be innocent or guilty?**

- Technically, I would be guilty, but there's no way God would send me to hell.

- **Why do you think that?**

- Whatever sins I've done, none of them deserves eternal punishment. Think about it, how can sixty or seventy years of sin deserve never-ending hell?

- **Okay, that's a fair question. How long do you think it takes to commit a murder?**

- I don't know.

- **Let's say we give the person a month to plan it and carry it out. That's one month to do the crime. Do you think they should only be imprisoned for one month?**

- Of course not.

- **So, the length of time to commit the crime is not the issue, the severity of the crime is what determines the punishment, wouldn't you agree?**

- Well, yes, but I don't see how my sins are severe enough to deserve eternal punishment.

- **The problem is that no criminal can decide his own sentence, it's up to the judge to do that, and in our case the judge is God. He states that your sins are so serious that they deserve eternal punishment, and it's His verdict that matters.**

Now, while there are other issues at stake in some of these questions and on occasions more detailed answers are necessary, often the simple responses given above are sufficient.

The best strategy for answering any objection raised against a person's guilt or punishment is to *keep the person in court until their defence is silent*. The few examples I have given could be multiplied but the answer is always the same. Any defence that is offered by a sinner against God's verdict or sentencing must be tried by the principles of law.

Guilty people want Good News!

The greatest benefit of this approach is that it opens the door for the message of the gospel. When a person realises he is guilty before God, the gospel of God's grace becomes attractive. Having learned that they cannot merit salvation, people wonder how they can possibly obtain it. The good news of a substitute and a Saviour is the only answer to the problem, and we should use the law as the springboard into the gospel.[51]

Bringing conviction is the work of the Holy Spirit. However, the Spirit uses *means* to convict. Just as the gospel is the message through which sinners are *converted*, the law is that through which many are *convicted*. The condemnatory effect of law often prepares hearts to welcome the sweet relief of the gospel of Christ.

[51.] In chapter 5 I have included an illustration I often use to lead from the law into the gospel.

Chapter 4

FACING CHALLENGES

The woman said to Him, "Sir, I perceive that You are a prophet. Our fathers worshiped on this mountain, and you Jews say that in Jerusalem is the place where one ought to worship." Jesus said to her, "Woman, believe Me, the hour is coming when you will neither on this mountain, nor in Jerusalem, worship the Father. You worship what you do not know; we know what we worship, for salvation is of the Jews. But the hour is coming, and now is, when the true worshipers will worship the Father in spirit and truth; for the Father is seeking such to worship Him. God is Spirit, and those who worship Him must worship in spirit and truth." The woman said to Him, "I know that Messiah is coming" (who is called Christ). "When He comes, He will tell us all things." Jesus said to her, "I who speak to you am He." (John 4:19-26)

Evangelism can be scary, yet the anticipation is usually much worse than the experience itself. Thinking of reasons why evangelism is frightening is not difficult. We don't like to be thought strange, we fear rejection, we don't want to mess up, and we especially don't want to let the Lord down.

I was held back in personal evangelism for all of these reasons, especially the last one. I was afraid of challenges being raised which I couldn't answer. While I knew that the Bible was true, and that I was truly saved, I did not know how to deal with challenges or questions. Very often, through fear of not communicating the gospel *well*, I didn't communicate it *at all*. I was afraid of misrepresenting what I knew to be true, and I didn't want to let the Lord down.

When you speak of the Lord Jesus Christ to unsaved people you must remember that your perspective is very different from theirs. They have no personal knowledge of Him, and many have no positive thoughts about Him. We enter a battleground when we communicate the gospel. We engage directly in spiritual warfare, and are taking the risk of being maligned and mocked.

One of the New Testament illustrations of the Christian is that of a soldier. A soldier accepts the risk to himself for the benefit of the country he represents. In Philippians 1, the apostle Paul was incarcerated for the sake of the gospel, yet he rejoiced because these things had "actually turned out for the furtherance of the gospel" (v. 12). Through the providence of God the abuse he endured resulted in the advance of the gospel. Do not suppose that your stammering remarks, made in weakness, cannot be the means in the hand of God for blessing; they certainly can.

"God may use any means at his disposal, and all means are at his disposal."[52]

I remember hearing the story of a young man who was giving out gospel tracts. He was accosted by two (so-called) Jehovah's Witnesses. They tied the poor lad in knots with their streamlined arguments and slick presentation. However, during the exchange, the young Christian stated repeatedly that Thomas had called Jesus "My Lord and my God" (John 20:28). Afterwards the two Jehovah's Witnesses felt very smug, for they had certainly bested this young Christian. He, on the other hand, likely went home in deep distress, thinking he had let the Lord down. Later that evening the Jehovah's Witnesses remembered the words repeated to them. They turned to John 20 and soon found that they had no answer to the clear implication of Christ's deity. They brought their question to the local Kingdom Hall and spoke to someone with greater learning. He was no help to them. Eventually, through the clear testimony of that young believer, and the power of God's word, they both accepted the true identity of Christ, and trusted Him as their Saviour.

Sometimes our weakness can be the vehicle for God's blessing. However, this does not remove from us the responsibility to seek answers for the challenges we may face.

[52.] Douglas Groothuis, *Christian Apologetics: A Comprehensive Case for Biblical Faith,* InterVarsity Press, 2011, p. 71.

Attitudes

When responding to a challenge, *what we say* is obviously vitally important. Yet, *how we say it* is also of great importance. Many a sincere questioner has been put off by a bad attitude. When Peter encouraged his readers to "always be ready to give a defense", he reminded them of the importance of their demeanour by adding, "with meekness and fear" (1 Pet. 3:15). Paul likewise stressed the importance of maintaining a fitting attitude: "Let your speech always be with grace, seasoned with salt, that you may know how you ought to answer each one" (Col. 4:6). In considering the Lord's response to challenges we discover that there are some attitudes which we should not adopt:

Don't be Evasive

I was asked in a question and answer session if I believed it was wise to respond to the challenges and questions of atheists. My response was that it was not only wise but essential. How would an atheist be persuaded of the truth if I refused to engage with him?

This question reflects a sincerely-held, but little-thought-out, view of evangelism. One Christian, while sharing the gospel, was faced with the challenge, "I just don't believe the Bible, so your message has no relevance to me." He responded, "Well, if you don't believe the Bible, then I have nothing to say to you. Goodbye."

Think carefully about that. Every atheist, agnostic, Muslim, Hindu, Buddhist, or animist, along with many nominal Christians, could have said, "I just don't believe the Bible, so your message has no relevance to me." Does that mean we truly have no responsibility toward them? Is the most loving approach to such a person to say goodbye? If this response is the best we can give, the only people we should share the gospel with are those who already believe the Bible to be the word of God. That will certainly restrict our outreach.

Such thinking cannot be accepted. We are responsible to reach every person with the gospel, and if that person is a Muslim, an atheist, or a Hindu, we are to take their challenges seriously, and we are to assist them towards a proper appreciation of God's word and of the gospel. With that in mind, notice how the Lord responded to the challenge raised by the woman of Samaria.

Her conscience having been aroused by the Lord's reminder of her sin, the woman said:

> *Sir, I perceive that You are a prophet. Our fathers worshiped on this mountain, and you Jews say that in Jerusalem is the place where one ought to worship.* (John 4:19-20)

Why did she begin to speak about worship? The flow of the conversation is suddenly interrupted by an apparently irrelevant subject. For most of us, a sudden question about worship when we have been driving home the problem of sin may seem like a diversionary tactic. Some do suggest that this woman was trying to wriggle off the hook – perhaps feeling uncomfortable with the direction of the conversation, she diverts onto safer ground. This is possible, of course, but I don't believe it to be the reason. In my view, her reason for asking about worship was that she had a genuine difficulty. Remember the circumstance of this exchange:

1. As a Samaritan, she had serious differences of doctrine with the Jews.

2. The man to whom she spoke was a Jew. He was not merely a Jew though, He had also shown prophetic insight by revealing details of her past life.

3. As a Jewish prophet, He could surely be called upon to answer a question of deep religious significance: Who is right, Samaritan or Jew?

Here the Lord was faced with a subject which was undoubtedly a genuine issue for which the woman was seeking an answer.

To bring the question into more familiar surroundings: suppose you were speaking to a Roman Catholic colleague about the gospel. You speak of the seriousness of sin and impress upon her the need of forgiveness. You then tell her about the forgiveness you enjoy for every sin you have committed. She replies by saying she can also receive forgiveness, but she gets hers differently. She must go to confession and tell a priest about her sins and he will absolve her of her guilt. She then asks: Who is right, my church or you?

Your colleague is not trying to change the subject, she is raising an issue with deeply significant implications for the discussion. In the same way, the Samaritan woman introduces a subject which troubles her, about which an answer is required so that she can rightly respond to the message she has heard. The Lord knows that the challenge is genuine, so He does not avoid it. "False ideas are the greatest obstacles to the reception of the gospel."[53] While we cannot be distracted by every matter raised, genuine questions must be answered, for otherwise they will form a roadblock to progress. Sometimes people have emotional barriers; for others the barriers are intellectual. It is our responsibility to attempt to remove any obstacles to enable progress towards the understanding of the truth.

Always remember that *a genuine question deserves a good answer*. The apostle Peter urged believers to "sanctify the Lord God in your hearts, and always be ready to give a defense to everyone who asks you a reason for the hope that is in you, with meekness and fear" (1 Pet. 3:15).

I have heard it said that the only message we have for sinners is the gospel. If what is meant is that only the gospel brings salvation, then there can be no argument. However, if the meaning is that we should not talk to unbelievers about anything else, that is manifestly false. The Lord Jesus had many conversations while here upon earth. A small fraction of them are recorded for us in the Gospels. Below is a list of some subjects He conversed with unbelievers about:

[53.] Moreland, *Love Your God With All Your Mind*, loc. 1337.

- Fasting
- John the Baptist
- Fulfilled Prophecy
- The Sabbath Day
- His Authority

- Traditions
- Taxation
- Divorce
- Resurrection
- Worship

Why did the Lord speak to sinners about these subjects? Because they were raised as issues and He deemed them worthy of reply. A Christian, earnestly sharing the gospel with an unbeliever, asked him some questions. The unbeliever answered his questions, then asked a question of his own. The Christian responded, "That's irrelevant!" The unbeliever replied, "How come when *you* ask something it's relevant and when *I* ask something it's irrelevant?" He had a point.

In John 4, the subject of worship is introduced by the woman, and the Lord sets out to answer her challenge. How did He respond?

Woman, believe Me, the hour is coming when you will neither on this mountain, nor in Jerusalem, worship the Father. You worship what you do not know; we know what we worship, for salvation is of the Jews. But the hour is coming, and now is, when the true worshipers will worship the Father in spirit and truth; for the Father is seeking such to worship Him. God is Spirit, and those who worship Him must worship in spirit and truth. (vv. 21-24)

This response deals with worship in some detail. While it is not our intention to look at that subject, we can draw some lessons from the way in which the Lord responded to her.[54]

Don't be Aggressive

It is far better to lose an argument and win a soul than to win an argument and lose a soul. Answering aggressively may serve to silence the opposition, but rarely to convince them. Draw a lesson from the famous statement of Erasmus: "It's no great feat to burn a little man, it is a great achievement to persuade him".[55] The Lord did not go on the attack by undermining the validity of the question, or treating it as foolish or unworthy of serious discussion. Even when a question appears foolish we should be respectful in our reply.

I have often been told that the only answer to give an atheist is to tell him that he is a fool. I have even been told to call him a liar. While I do not doubt that an atheist is both foolish and self-deceived, yet scriptures used to prove these points are not intended to give instruction for evangelism.[56] If you insist that the proper approach to an atheist is to call him a fool, remember that you must figure out a way of doing so *graciously* for we are commanded: "Let your speech always be with grace, seasoned with salt, that you may know how you ought to answer each one" (Col. 4:6).

[54.] The second part of the book will deal more comprehensively with common challenges to the gospel.

[55.] Erasmus, cited in Os Guinness, *Fool's Talk: Recovering the Art of Christian Persuasion*, InterVarsity Press, 2015.

[56.] cf. Ps. 14:1; 53:1; Rom. 1:18-21.

Ask yourself the question: how would the conversation go after you called a person a fool or a liar? How would you react if *he* called *you* a fool or a liar? Would you not be offended? Would you be likely to listen to his message? Our speech must always be gracious, even though we must never be less than honest. Tactfulness and truthfulness can co-exist.

A simple principle to keep in mind is:

Always make it your goal to keep your conversations cordial. Sometimes that will not be possible. If a principled, charitable expression of your ideas makes someone mad, there's little you can do about it. Jesus' teaching made some people furious. Just make sure it's your ideas that offend and not you, that your beliefs cause the dispute and not your behavior.[57]

Don't be Negative

Those who engage in the battle for souls can become a little cynical. Sometimes we assume that a person is asking a question insincerely and on occasion we may have good ground to think this. However, if there is any doubt at all, we should give the benefit of the doubt.

The Lord knew the motives of every person with whom He spoke. He "knew all men, and had no need that anyone should testify of man, for He knew what was in man" (John 2:24-25). The motives of sinful people are *never* completely pure, and yet the Lord did not fail to answer

---

[57.] Koukl, *Tactics*, p. 31. Emphasis his.

the questions put to Him. There were occasions when He challenged the motives of His listeners. For the most part, however, He entered into conversation in good faith, treating people as genuine participants in the discussion.

We do not have the insight of the Lord Jesus and, as a rule, we are very poor judges of motives. Unless it is very evident that a person is asking questions with malicious or dishonest intent, we should give them the benefit of the doubt and answer in good faith. If we do assume impure motives in a sincere questioner, we may make a very costly mistake.

Don't be Naive

Sometimes it will become evident that the person is not sincere. This can be discerned in several ways. They may show themselves unwilling to listen to your responses or to answer your questions. They may raise questions which are clearly irrelevant or foolish. They may begin to attack you verbally without cause.

When a person is insincere, there is no value in shutting your eyes to the facts. The Lord was confronted by those who were ultimately seeking His destruction, and He "perceived their craftiness" (Luke 20:23).

Those who belong to the cults are particularly adept at raising issues for the express purpose of knocking conversation off track. Their tactics remind me of my treatment of a pet cat when I was a young boy. Someone showed me the effect a laser pointer had on a cat, and you can imagine the rest: the poor creature went tearing around the house chasing an evasive point of light. At the end, it was a shaking, bewildered, twitching wreck. Conversations with cultists can feel a bit like this, and control needs to be exercised on your part so that you do not become their source of amusement.

In conversation with cultists who profess faith in the Bible, there comes a point when they are confronted with the truth, and it is then that their insincerity often becomes clear. Suddenly they throw in a random or controversial subject with the intent of deflecting you and escaping truth. It is important in these circumstances to remain civil and calm. However, this is not the same as being putty in the hands of an opponent. The best way to react to this is to gently but firmly state that you will answer their new question *after* you have concluded dealing with the present subject of conversation. You can even communicate this very positively: "You've already raised an excellent question, and I'd like to give you the best answer I can for that. I'll deal with that next subject after I conclude, thanks." If they become unreasonable and are no longer willing participants in conversation, just finish off politely, "I don't think we're making any headway here, but I'd love to chat to you again sometime. Would that be possible?" As Newman says, "Until someone is more interested in truth than in airing his or her own opinions, it's best to talk about the weather."[58]

This simple tactic means that you remain in control, the ball is back in their court, and the heat of the

---

[58.] Randy Newman, *Questioning Evangelism: Engaging People's Hearts the Way Jesus Did*, Kregel, 2010, p. 45.

immediate conflict can die away. If they are sincere, they will happily allow you to conclude or arrange another occasion to meet.

Remaining calm and leaving on good terms is important. The door is thereby left open for further contact. Perhaps they will be more receptive on another occasion.

Don't be Deceptive

God is not well represented by those who put words into His mouth, but for many of us there is a real temptation to do this. At the root of our fallen nature is the sin of pride. When a challenge is raised that we are not prepared for, we don't want to look less than omniscient, so we are tempted to make up an answer. While the words "I don't know" seem to stick in our throats, they are much to be preferred to our inventing an answer.

The Lord, of course, did not make up His answer on the spur of the moment. He who is "the truth" (John 14:6) was ever truthful in His speech. He could say "the word which you hear is not Mine but the Father's who sent Me" (John 14:24). If the Lord faithfully declared the word of the Father, should we not do the same?

Paul, reminding the Thessalonians of his arrival among them with the gospel, wrote: "our exhortation did not come from error or uncleanness, nor was it in deceit. But as we have been approved by God to be entrusted with the gospel, even so we speak, not as pleasing men, but God who tests our hearts" (1 Thess. 2:3-4). There was no error in the content of Paul's message. He remembered always that the gospel was entrusted to him, and he was not at liberty to tamper with it.

How did Paul answer challenges to the gospel on this occasion? He "reasoned with them from the Scriptures, explaining and demonstrating that the Christ had to suffer and rise again from the dead, and saying, 'This Jesus whom I preach to you is the Christ.'" (Acts 17:2-3). Paul's answers had the rock-solid foundation of Holy Scripture.

As those who are "ambassadors for Christ" (2 Cor. 5:20) our words must be drawn from God's word. This does not mean that every answer must be a direct quotation of scripture, but that the Bible rightly interpreted must inform all our answers. If you do not know the answer, do not generate one.

To widen the point, there should be no deception of any kind in our evangelism. Paul not only knew that his message was free from error, he goes on to show that his motives were pure and his methods involved no trickery. Sadly, many cultists and atheists do not feel such constraints upon them. Such hold on to their viewpoint at all costs, even if that means relegating truth to the dustbin. We should not be like this, for we have no authority that competes with God's word. We cannot twist scripture; we cannot insert our ideas into the text; we must not allow our pride to rob us of the high ground of communicating only the truth.

While it is true that a genuine question deserves a good answer, it is necessary to "know from the start that we can never give complete and convincing answers to every question".[59] The reasons for this are at least two-fold. First, we are not omniscient, and second, God has allowed some mysteries to remain as such. He has not chosen to give the reason why, or the logic behind every circumstance or fact. While we can freely acknowledge that we do not know everything, we can faithfully acknowledge that we do know enough. Scripture is not exhaustive in its revelation, but it is sufficient.

To summarise: when we experience opposition, or a challenge is raised, our attitude must show that we care for the challenger, value the opportunity given to converse, and hold truth in the highest regard.

Answers

While a proper attitude is essential, it is insufficient on its own. A good attitude should provide support for a good answer. Having considered the attitude of Christ, we must now learn from His answer.

An Available answer

The Lord was ready with an answer, and so should we be (cf. Col. 4:6; 1 Pet. 3:15). None of us will have answers to every question, but we should prepare ourselves to answer questions which are commonly asked. We are not all-knowing but we have the word of God to make us "thoroughly equipped for every good work" (2 Tim. 3:17).

[59.] Guinness, *Fool's Talk*. pp. 37-38.

Paul, in his letter to the Philippians, speaks of himself as being "appointed for the defense of the gospel" (1:17). The word Paul uses was often used in a court of law to signify a *speech made in defence*. The gospel is being judged every day in the court of public opinion. The charges against it are many; they include the accusations that it is unreliable and irrelevant. Every person in society hears these accusations because they are propagated on mainstream media. You, on the other hand, know that the gospel is innocent of the charges placed against it. When you speak with someone about the gospel, your speech in defence of it is possibly the only defence they will hear. Can you give a good defence of the gospel?

If you were accused of a crime you did not commit, and had to appear before a court to defend yourself, there is little doubt that you would prepare well for the occasion. Rather than arrive in court unrehearsed, you would anticipate the cross-examination and equip yourself to meet it. Your preparation would be thorough, because you care about the verdict of the court. Don't forget that you *should* care, both about the reputation of the gospel and the salvation of souls. In the small courtroom of your one-to-one conversation with an unbeliever you should be prepared to defend the gospel.

An Authoritative answer

There is a world of difference between authority and aggression. To shout the loudest is not to win the argument. In fact, one indication that a person is uncomfortable with their position, is on the defensive, or fears a challenge, is that they become more assertive. The story is told of someone who lifted the Bible of a preacher and leafed through the pages which contained many sermon notes. After a while, he came to a little marginal note which read, "Shout here! Point weak."[60]

The Lord showed no aggression, but He did speak with authority. He said, "Woman, believe me," and proceeded to make definite statements which communicated with great clarity the answer to her question. As the omniscient Lord, there was no question of Christ's authority. With us, however, speaking authoritatively on a subject is only possible if we are speaking in accordance with God's word. When the Bible speaks with clarity on a subject, we should show our confidence in God's revelation by communicating it with conviction.

Very often, the questions that are raised in everyday evangelism are answered easily from scripture. Biblical illiteracy is the cause of many foolish questions. People may raise ethical points, religious issues, personal problems, or emotional difficulties, which flow from a misunderstanding of scripture. An assured, straightforward explanation of the scriptural position on these issues is generally sufficient. When the Lord was challenged, He often showed His confidence in God's word by asking, "Have you not read ...?"[61]

[60.] S. Lewis Johnson, from the transcript of the sermon *The Days of Noah*, http://www.sljinstitute.net/pentateuch/genesis/the-day-of-noah/.

[61.] Matt. 12:3, 5; 19:4; 22:31; Mark 12:10, 26; Luke 6:3.

One day I got chatting to Adrian, a young man of seventeen who was still attending high school. I asked him if he believed in God and he said that he did, and that he attended a Scripture Union group in school. However, he was not a Christian. When I asked him why he was not a Christian, he said that there were parts of the Bible that he did not believe. I enquired what parts he meant, and he replied: "I don't believe all that stuff about God hating blacks and gays." Adrian was not raising hot-button topics for fun; he truly thought the Bible said God hated black people and homosexual people. I told him I would deal with each of his issues in turn because they were very different. He listened as I showed him from Acts 17 that God had made "from one blood every nation of men to dwell on all the face of the earth" (v. 26). I told him that every person was made in the image of God, and was valuable in God's sight. I told him of sin's effect upon all, and the work of Christ for all. Having ascertained that he understood that, I began to address the thorny issue of homosexual practice. To do so I showed him from Genesis 2 that God had instituted marriage, that He clearly intended a heterosexual union, and that *every* sexual relationship outside of God's ideal of marriage was therefore sinful. I explained that homosexual acts are sinful, yet the Bible recorded in 1 Corinthians 6 that people who practised these very sins had been saved. I quoted John 3:16 to leave him in no doubt of God's love for all humanity, then applied the matter to him by using the law (see the previous chapter).

The important point to notice here is that no *apology* was needed for what the scripture said, but an *apologetic* was required to clarify and present it fairly. Obstacles need to be cleared from the path before the cross can be reached. Very often the proper contextualisation of the biblical record provides all the defence that is necessary.

It is crucial to communicate confidence in God's word for, if you don't show confidence in it, why expect them to believe it? Faith "comes by hearing, and hearing by the word of God" (Rom. 10:17). When Paul arrived in Thessalonica, the gospel "did not come … in word only, but also in power, and in the Holy Spirit and in much assurance" (1 Thess. 1:5). He and his fellow evangelists preached with great conviction in the truth of God's word. The result was that the Thessalonians "welcomed it not as the word of men, but as it is in truth, the word of God" (2:13). It is important to communicate our confidence in God's word, because confidence can be contagious.

Because of our limited knowledge, there are questions we will not be able to answer with certainty. However, when it comes to matters about which the Bible is clear we should not be ambiguous. We should not speak as those who have merely weighed up probabilities and are taking the best bet; we should convey calm assured confidence in the scriptures. We should never be tempted to change the message of scripture even if people reject it or are offended by it. To quote MacArthur, "If the truth offends, then let it offend. People have been living their whole lives in offense to God; let them be offended for a while".[62]

[62.] John MacArthur, *Found: God's Will: Find the Direction and Purpose God wants for your Life*, David C Cook, 2012, p. 63.

An Adequate answer

The Lord's answer dealt directly with the issue that was raised and provided sufficient information to satisfy the questioner. While we have a direction to maintain, we must also truly address that which is hindering concentration on the gospel, or reception of the Saviour. The Lord was confronted with the issue of worship and it is worship with which He dealt.

The Lord addressed the subject of worship in a manner that enabled Him to disclose further truth about God. Two of the most significant revelations in scripture concerning God are given in this short section.[63] While this is not the place for a detailed consideration of these, it is surely worthy of note that in Jesus' response He not only fully addressed the issue that was raised but used the opportunity to disclose further truth about the God He had come to reveal (cf. John 1:18).

Not only so, but, using the revelation of the true God as a springboard, the Lord showed that her thoughts about worship were wrong. She said, "Our fathers worshiped on this mountain, and you Jews say that in Jerusalem is the place where one ought to worship" (v. 20). The Lord responded, "The hour is coming when you will neither on this mountain, nor in Jerusalem, worship the Father" (v. 21). Evidently the place of worship was to be of little concern. Rather, "the hour is coming, and now is, when the true worshipers will worship the Father in spirit and truth ... those who worship Him must worship in spirit and

---

[63.] The repeated term "the Father" (vv. 21, 23) and the declaration "God is spirit" (v. 24).

truth" (vv. 23-24). The people who worship and the nature of their worship were the all-important matters. It is *true* worshippers He seeks, and such must "worship in spirit and in truth". Worship is to be both *sincere* and *scriptural*. Samaritans may have been enthusiastic worshippers, but their worship was not properly informed. Jews had the divine revelation of God in their scriptures, but Judaism had become the epitome of deadness and barrenness (cf. v. 22). Neither enthusiastic heresy nor barren orthodoxy is acceptable to God.

The Lord immediately drew the woman away from what divided Jews and Samaritans to what really mattered, a genuine relationship with God, for, "the Father is seeking such to worship Him" (v. 23). Truth about God was revealed and the nature of acceptable worship was made known. He communicated God's desire for true worshippers. This was intended to further convict her of sin and to deepen her longing after God.

A most important aspect of gospel communication is to properly represent God. *Challenges often enable us to do this.* Allowing questions grants opportunity to reveal more fully the God and Father of the Lord Jesus Christ. We should learn to use such opportunities for this purpose.

Arguments

While we are made in the image of God, the Fall has given us an inclination to reject truth rather than rejoice in it. As a result, many gospel conversations will not be a simple communication of divine truth without interruption or resistance. God's first evangelistic communication with fallen man met with resistance. When God said to Adam, "Have you eaten from the tree of which I commanded you that you should not eat?" (Gen. 3:11), Adam responded, "The woman whom You gave to be with me, she gave me of the tree, and I ate" (v. 12). Man's first response to the convicting voice of God was to engineer a way to avoid admitting personal culpability. Adam blamed Eve, and through Eve he pointed the finger at God.

Man is still the same. Whatever the excuse for unbelief, we can be sure that there is, lurking under the surface, wilful resistance.

> We should ... never view unbelief as flatly theoretical, loftily neutral or merely as a worldview that people just happen to have. However suave and cool its attitudes, and however rational its arguments may sometimes appear to be, unbelief is different in its heart. Deep down, the unbelieving heart is active, wilful, deliberate, egotistic, devious, scheming, and unrelenting in its open refusal, its deliberate rebellion and its total resistance to God and the full truth of his reality ... "[64]

It is for this reason that "it can never be countered by purely intellectual arguments that ignore the power of the dark secret of this heart."[65]

While this is so, many are so self-deceived that they believe they have good *reason* to reject God's truth. Rather

---

[64.] Guinness, *Fools Talk*, p. 94.
[65.] Ibid., p. 94.

than giving God the glory He is due, and responding in gratitude to His many blessings, men have become "futile in their thoughts" and their "foolish hearts" have become darkened. "Professing to be wise, they became fools" (Rom. 1:21-22).

How can we expose to such that their unbelief is not merely intellectual but volitional? If people live in constant denial of reality, how can we cause them to face up to it? One way to do this is to present evidence and arguments that positively support the truth we teach.[66] This the Lord did on more than one occasion.[67] Another very effective way to do so is to undermine the confidence that the unbeliever has in his own assertions. This is often an essential part of evangelism. Just as weeds require removal before seeds are planted, so false ideas need to be uprooted before the good word of the gospel can bring forth fruit. Some easily mastered tactics greatly assist in this work:

Take it for a Ride

It can be very enlightening to take a claim or challenge for a test-drive to show where it leads. The Lord Jesus was often confronted by religious opponents. Pharisees and Sadducees, scribes and lawyers all sought to undermine His ministry and to attack His person. In Matthew 12 a very

---

[66] The maxim "Convince a man against his will, he's of the same opinion still" is true. However, we must also remember that the will is informed by the intellect and by the emotions. Therefore, in appealing to the intellect or emotions a person's will can be influenced. Ultimately, whatever evidence is given, whatever appeals are made, whatever plausible rationale is presented, the individual can wilfully resist the truth.

[67] See the second part of this book.

severe accusation was made after He had exercised divine authority in the expulsion of a demon:

> *Now when the Pharisees heard it they said, "This fellow does not cast out demons except by Beelzebub, the ruler of the demons." But Jesus knew their thoughts, and said to them: "Every kingdom divided against itself is brought to desolation, and every city or house divided against itself will not stand. If Satan casts out Satan, he is divided against himself. How then will his kingdom stand?* (vv. 24-26)

The Pharisees show the depth of their ill feeling toward the Lord. Rather than rejoice in the deliverance of someone from the power of Satan, they used the good work of Jesus to accuse Him of being in league with the devil. The Lord responds using a tactic known by the Latin term *reductio ad absurdum*. He caused the accusation of His opponents to appear foolish.

The ridiculous accusation of the Pharisees was that Jesus had been casting out demons with the authority and power of Beelzebub, the prince of the demons. The Lord takes their accusation to its absurd logical conclusion: Satan must be intent on destroying his own kingdom if he is casting out his own forces. His accusers are faced with the folly of their challenge.

The Pharisees' challenge was *taken for a ride*. It was driven to its logical destination and it arrived in absurdity. The foolish conclusion exposed the foolish challenge.

The Lord's goal in using this tactic was to assist His accusers and others to accept the truth of His person. If the Lord was truly casting out demons, as they admitted He was, and if it was illogical to claim that He was doing so for Satan, what is the alternative? There is only one other option available to the Jewish mind: He was acting for God. For the Lord, using logic was not a means to "win battles, but to achieve understanding or insight in his hearers".[68]

This tactic is of tremendous assistance when sharing the gospel. Often, rather than directly opposing a challenge, it is helpful to say, "Well, let us suppose that is true for a moment, then ...". This is inoffensive as you are genuinely considering the claim that has been made, but the conclusion drawn is always absurd. Consider the following example:

Our best is good enough

The challenge: "I think we get to heaven by doing the best we can."

People who believe in heaven often assume that they will one day be there. When asked why they suppose this to be the case, the most common response is: "Because I'm a good person." If pressed about how good they would need to be to earn a place in heaven, they often reply, "As long as I do the best I can, I'll get in." The implication is that it would be unfair of God to turn them away – no one can do better than their best.

[68.] Dallas Willard, *Jesus the Logician*, cited in Douglas Groothuis, *On Jesus*, Wadsworth Philosophers Series, Wadsworth, 2003, p. 23.

Think carefully through this challenge. What is the standard that must be reached to get to heaven? I must do the best I can. What does this really mean? It means that at every moment of life, in every decision of life, I could not have done better. It means that I have always been as kind, caring, compassionate, honest, upright, faithful, and pure as it was possible for me to be.

The major problem is that no one has ever lived like this.[69] I certainly haven't. Have you? Do you know of *anyone* who can honestly say that they have done their best? Of course not. The logical conclusion drawn from the challenge is that no one will ever be in heaven.

The person who holds to this idea has not thought through the implications. You must help them to do so. If you do, they will soon see that the conclusion is not what they anticipated.

Our natural tendency is to disagree with the challenge. We want to say, "That's not right." Sometimes it is far more powerful to *show* a person that they are not right than to merely *say* that they are not right. In fact, there is nothing more effective for encouraging a person to rethink his position than to show him not only that his challenge *is* not right but that it *cannot possibly* be right because it leads to an absurd, and foolish, conclusion.

The next time someone disagrees with the way of salvation, rather than arguing with him and coming to an impasse, why not take his side and say, "Okay, let's look at

---

[69] Apart from the Lord Jesus.

it your way," and draw out the implications of his position by taking his claim for a ride.

Suicide

The law of non-contradiction states that "Nothing can both be and not be at the same time in the same respect"[70]. This law, first codified by Aristotle but certainly not invented by him, is basic to all our reasoning abilities. When the Lord set one option over against another in opposition, as He often did, He was giving implicit credence to this law of logic.

This law gives birth to a couple of very useful tactics for personal evangelism. The first has been called the suicide tactic.[71] To commit suicide is to kill yourself – to fall on your own sword. Many arguments presented by those who challenge the gospel do just this. They are self-destructive because they are self-refuting. They are self-refuting because, if they are true, then they are false. They *contradict* themselves. When a person makes a claim of this nature, your job is to point out the contradiction and watch the claim self-destruct before their eyes. Let us take a couple of examples:

The truth is there is no truth

The challenge: "There is no truth," or "We can't know the truth."

This challenge has become more popular as society has become more pluralistic. It may not always be expressed as directly as this, however, many hold a postmodern view of

---

[70.] Aristotle, cited in Groothuis, *Christian Apologetics*, p. 46.
[71.] cf. Koukl, *Tactics*, p. 107.

truth which implies either that there is no absolute truth, or, if there is, there is no way of knowing it.

On this view, in place of objective truth, people have their personal truth — *You have your truth and I have my truth*. This springs from the notion that every person's view of reality is equally valid. If this is so, then *none* of them are valid because, once all beliefs are accepted as equally true, none can be objectively true, because they refute each other.[72]

People have taken refuge in uncertainty. When what you say challenges their beliefs, they respond: "There's no such a thing as truth," or "We can't possibly know truth." However, there is a *contradiction* implicit in this: they believe that their own statement is true. And they want you to accept it as true. In effect, they are saying — *The absolute truth is – there is no absolute truth*. There can be no more contradictory statement than this. If it is true, then it is also false.

But how can you respond to such a statement? Suppose in conversation with a person, you begin to stress the truth-claims of the gospel. Her response is to say, "There's no such a thing as truth." You could gently respond with a question: "Do you believe *that's* the truth?" If the challenge is, "We can't know the truth," your response could be, "But how do you know *that's* the truth?"

Always keep in mind that you want to win the soul, not just the argument, so these tactics should be used graciously.

---

[72] cf. Barrs, *The Heart of Evangelism*, pp. 149-154.

The intent is not to humiliate anyone but to help them see the contradictory nature of their beliefs. Your ultimate goal is to lead them to the One who said, "I am ... the truth" (John 14:6).

You're wrong for saying I'm wrong

The challenge: "It's wrong to push your morality on anyone else!"

This objection is popular because people dislike being held accountable to any standard outside themselves. If beauty is in the eye of the beholder, so is morality.

Of course, the challenge suffers once again from deep internal inconsistency. This person believes that no one should tell anyone else that what they are doing is wrong. However, *they* are telling *you* that what you are doing is wrong. The challenge is — *It's wrong to say anything is wrong.*

This therefore contains a practical contradiction. If the person said nothing, he could hold this view without contradiction, but when he expresses this view, he immediately falls under his own condemnation. He is making a moral judgment while denying you the right to do so. *If his statement is right, then he is wrong for making it.*

Once again, the response to this statement is to ask a question. Suppose you are applying the law, and a person begins to feel its convicting power; they might respond with, "You can't tell anyone what's right or wrong." Your answer could be "Are you saying it's *wrong* for me to do so?" This may need to be restated a few times before your challenger picks up on what he has been doing.

The way to deal with such statements is to calmly and gently point out the inconsistency and watch the challenge self-destruct.

Homicide

Following the same principle as the previous tactic, the Homicide tactic is utilised when two or more contradictory ideas are expressed during the course of a conversation. While any one statement of the challenger may stand on its own merit, yet there are inconsistencies when his statements are considered together. One idea kills another idea; it commits *homicide*. The following examples may be helpful:

To Judge or not to judge

During your conversation, the following two claims are made:

1. "If your God is so good, why does He not judge the evil in the world?"

2. "Your God is cruel for destroying the Canaanites in the Old Testament."

These objections to God's character are often raised. While they have always been around, they have been popularised in recent decades by the writings of some very prominent atheists. Notice the inconsistency.

First, God's goodness is challenged because He *doesn't* punish sin. Then, a short while later, His goodness is challenged because He *does* punish sin. As we can see, this puts God in a no-win situation as far as this challenger is concerned. If God punishes sin He's evil, and if He doesn't He's evil.

If this kind of thing happens in conversation, you must make it very clear that your challenger cannot have it both ways. He can choose to retain one of his objections, but he cannot keep them both. Once this is pointed out, while some may bluster and deny any contradiction, many will recognise the point and settle for one objection. You have halved your problem.

Moralising without morality

Another favourite is below:

1. "There is no such thing as objective morality."

2. "Your God is evil for allowing suffering in the world."

Here the claim is first made that *evil does not really exist*; it is merely a human construct, or it is a subjective matter. However, in the second claim it is assumed that *evil does really exist*, for God is accused of being evil. The contradiction then is evident. This challenger believes, according to his convenience, that evil *does not* exist and that evil *does* exist.

To utilise the homicide tactic effectively, you must point out that the arguments cancel each other out. Your opponent can hold one belief, but not both. This won't remove both challenges but it will leave you with only one to answer.

Are Answers Enough?

At this point we should be convinced of our responsibility to answer genuine intellectual challenges raised against the gospel. However, many issues are not merely intellectual; they are intensely emotional. As someone has put it, "There are armchair sufferers and wheelchair sufferers."[73]

Bronagh came running down her path as I attempted to open her gate to give her John's Gospel. She asked me what I was giving out. When I told her, her eyes clouded: "I'm not sure if I believe in God." I asked her what it was that caused her to doubt God's existence. She replied: "Why would God make people commit suicide?"

It was immediately clear that this was not a general question about suffering; it was a personal question about suicide. When someone begins to speak personally about very painful issues, we must treat them as we would like to be treated. Some have deep emotional wounds which are sensitive to the touch. Failure to be sensitive and gentle will cause them to retreat from you.

"That's a good question. Why would you ask that?" I said. She informed me that her son, her brother, and her nephew had all taken their own lives recently. She was in terrible emotional pain. My response was simply, "I'm so sorry to hear that; I can't imagine what you've gone through." I could have wept with her. As the conversation proceeded slowly, I carefully communicated one major point: denying God's existence would not remove her pain,

---

[73] Paul Williams, *Intentional: Evangelism That Takes People To Jesus*, 10publishing, 2016, p. 92.

for God alone could bring comfort to her and give purpose to what had happened. She listened and accepted a copy of John's Gospel. I returned at a later date with a little booklet on suffering which further explained the gospel.

Bronagh did not want or need an intellectual argument giving reasons for her relatives' suicide and her own suffering. She needed to be comforted, and she needed to be convinced that God cared. We can only help in these circumstances if we properly represent God and reflect His love in our own attitude.[74]

Facing challenges is undoubtedly the aspect of evangelism which people fear most. However, if we maintain the right attitude, and master the arguments, we will have little to fear.

---

[74] For more on the emotional problem of suffering see chapter 9.

Chapter 5

PREACHING CHRIST

Opening conversation and controlling it, reaching the sinner's conscience, answering challenges – these are all vital aspects of evangelism. But preaching Christ makes a conversation truly evangelistic. This is the goal toward which all our conversations should be directed. Not every conversation will reach this target, but every conversation should be with a view to sharing the gospel in its fullness with the sinner. Evangelism is, as we have defined it, *telling sinners the gospel so that they may be saved.*

How did the Lord Jesus communicate the gospel to the woman of Samaria? Notice the essential elements of His message, His approach to her, and the responsibility He placed upon her. We will now examine these vital subjects.

Jesus answered and said to her, "If you knew the gift of God, and who it is who says to you, 'Give Me a drink,' you would have asked Him, and He would have given you living water." (John 4:10)

Jesus answered and said to her, "Whoever drinks of this water will thirst again, but whoever drinks of the water that I shall give him will never thirst. But the water that I shall give him will become in him a fountain of water springing up into everlasting life." (vv. 13-14)

The woman said to Him, "I know that Messiah is coming" (who is called Christ). "When He comes, He will tell us all things." Jesus said to her, "I who speak to you am He." (vv. 25-26)

Gospel Content

If someone were to ask you, "What is the gospel?", how would you respond? Many verses in scripture summarise the main points, and these should be memorized. The gospel consists of good news of which God is the source (Rom. 1:1; 15:16) and Christ is the theme (Mark 1:1; Rom. 1:3-4, 9). The intended beneficiaries of the gospel are sinners (Rom. 1:16-17; Eph. 1:13). As we consider how the Lord presented the gospel in John 4, these facts are foremost.

He said, "If you knew the gift of God, and who it is who says to you, 'Give Me a drink,' you would have asked Him, and He would have given you living water" (v. 10). Here we have salvation presented as the "gift of God", available through Christ, and accessible to this sinful woman.

God is the Source

"If you knew the gift of God" (v. 10). People are often deluded enough to think that they can choose their own method of salvation. This is because the postmodern mind-set leads to the rejection of any authority outside of self: my way of getting to heaven is right for me, because I am satisfied with it. However, this ignores the vital issue of *God* being satisfied with the way. We are not in the position to decide the way of salvation.

God's *righteousness* bars me from entering heaven based on my own performance. Paul's letter to the Romans eloquently summarises God's perspective on humanity:

"There is none righteous, no, not one;
There is none who understands;
There is none who seeks after God.
They have all turned aside;
They have together become unprofitable;
There is none who does good, no, not one."
"Their throat is an open tomb;
With their tongues they have practiced deceit";
"The poison of asps is under their lips";
"Whose mouth is full of cursing and bitterness."
"Their feet are swift to shed blood;
Destruction and misery are in their ways;
And the way of peace they have not known."
"There is no fear of God before their eyes."

Now we know that whatever the law says, it says to those who are under the law, that every mouth may be stopped, and all the world may become guilty before God. (Rom. 3:9-19)

This is God's view of the human family and, from His perspective, "there is no difference; for all have sinned and fall short of the glory of God" (vv. 22-23). As the righteous Judge, God owes to no one the offer of salvation. He is under no obligation to man whatsoever. He has given His law, and we have broken it; we are deserving of His judgment, and we have no right of appeal.

However, God's *grace* has met the demands of His righteousness, and salvation is now freely available as God's gift. Salvation is not a reward for the righteous, it is a gift for the guilty.[75] Paul, referring to those who stand guilty before God because of their sin, shows that they can be "justified freely by His grace through the redemption that is in Christ Jesus" (v. 24).

To be justified "freely" is to be declared righteous by God through no merit of our own. God has already assessed us as being guilty, so there is no reason *in us* for Him to declare us righteous. The cause for our justification is not in us, but *in Himself*; it is "by His grace". In spite of our lack of merit, God bestows upon us His favour, removing our guilt and giving us a status of righteousness before Him.

The story is told of a conference on comparative religions in which religious experts were debating what doctrine, if any, was unique to Christianity. C. S. Lewis was one of the attendees and, upon entering the room and learning of the debate, he responded: "Oh, that's easy. It's grace." After some further discussion, all were agreed: Christianity is

---

[75.] I have attempted to find the source of this quote and have not been able.

unique because in it salvation is by God's grace alone.[76]

Grace is kindness shown to the undeserving, and the "gospel of the grace of God" (Acts 20:24) is the tremendous news of God's kindness towards those who are hell-deserving. It is essential that we communicate this fact. Salvation is offered to us by God as a free gift for the simple reason that there is no possible way for us to earn it. What we have earned from God is His judgment; what we are offered by God is salvation: "For the wages of sin is death, but the gift of God is eternal life in Christ Jesus our Lord" (Rom. 6:23). God has taken the initiative or no salvation would be available. "For God so loved the world that He gave His only begotten Son, that whoever believes in Him should not perish but have everlasting life" (John 3:16).

Christ is the Theme

How can God do such a thing? How can a righteous judge acquit a guilty person? The only answer is: "through the redemption that is in Christ Jesus" (Rom. 3:24). Every crime against God deserves punishment. If God wants to righteously remove this punishment from us, the answer must be a willing substitute; and this substitute must be able to make the payment justice demands for our freedom. This brings us to the great theme of the gospel: the Lord Jesus Christ.

Throughout the New Testament, the constant theme of apostle and evangelist was Christ. Preaching the gospel

---

[76.] Philip Yancey, *Where Is God When It Hurts? / What's So Amazing About Grace?*, Two Books In One, Zondervan, 2009, p. 329.

was even referred to as preaching Christ.[77] The message the Lord communicated to the woman of Samaria was likewise the good news concerning Himself. Everything we have considered up to this point has been with this goal in view. We *must* preach Christ.

However, we must understand what it means to preach Christ. Evangelism consists of much more than an appeal to "trust Jesus". We must inform *about* Christ before we can invite *to* Him. The four Gospel narratives of the Bible are designed to introduce to us the person and work of Christ. The foundation of the gospel is the historical facts about the Lord Jesus and their doctrinal implications.

The gospel contains historical and propositional truth concerning the person and the work of the Lord, and this must be taught. During her dialogue with Jesus, the woman's understanding of His true identity progressed step-by-step. She spoke first of Him as a "Jew" (v. 9), then as a "prophet"[78] (v. 19), then as Messiah (vv. 25-26; 28-29). Ultimately, she recognised who the giver of salvation was (cf. v. 10), and enjoyed the gift that He freely offered (vv. 28-29). The reason for this increase in knowledge was that the woman was *instructed;* foundational truths about Christ were communicated to her. What the Lord taught was *truth* which enabled her to *trust*. "So then," Paul wrote to the

---

[77.] Acts 8:5. See also v. 35; 1 Cor. 1:23; 2 Cor. 4:5; Eph. 3:8; Php. 1:15-18; Col. 1:28.

[78.] D. A. Carson goes so far as to say that "the syntax of the Greek allows the translation 'I can see that you are *the* prophet.'" (D. A. Carson, *The Gospel According to John,* The Pillar New Testament Commentary, Eerdmans, 1991, p. 221). The point is that her recognition of the glory of Christ's person was increasing rapidly.

Roman Christians, "faith comes by hearing" (Rom. 10:17). The faith required for salvation is a response to revelation. As Schaeffer put it: "Knowledge precedes faith. This is crucial in understanding the Bible".[79] Revelation must be given before faith can be exercised.

James answered the knock on his door wearing only a pair of shorts, and holding a bottle. In his living room a group of his friends were drinking and doing drugs. James asked me what I was doing at his door and, when I told him, he invited me in. He ushered me into the kitchen and began his story: "I got saved just over three weeks ago. I was on a high for three weeks but now look at me!" He had evidently been drinking, but was well able to hold a conversation. I asked him how he had got saved. He said: "I met a Christian who invited me to hear the gospel. I went along and, during the appeal, my hand went up. Honestly, it went up all by itself! Then a lot of people gathered round me clapping me on the back, congratulating me for making the decision." He went on to expand upon his three weeks of being "saved" before looking ruefully at the bottle in his hand. "What happened?"

I told him that I wasn't in the business of telling people whether they were saved or not, but I wanted to tell him the gospel. I explained the problem of sin and traced the story of the Lord's coming into the world to save us. I began to speak of His death upon the cross, and James said, "But how could He have died on the cross for me? He didn't

---

[79.] Francis Schaeffer, *The God Who is There*, The Francis A. Schaeffer Trilogy, Crossway, 1990, p. 154.

even know me." Answering his question, I continued until I reached the point where I said: "The Bible says that, to be saved, a person must trust the Lord Jesus Christ to save them. Paul and Silas said, "Believe on the Lord Jesus Christ, and you will be saved" (Acts 16:31). Have you ever done that?" "No," he said with a blank expression, "never." "Well then," I concluded, "while I don't like to tell people if they're saved or not, the Bible makes it clear that without trusting Christ you can't be saved. So, James, I think you may take it that you're not saved."

James' problem was that he had no concept of the gospel. He neither knew what salvation was, nor who the Saviour was. Whatever response he made was uninformed and ineffectual. He was not saved.

The Lord showed that a proper understanding of His identity was essential for salvation in verse 10: "If you knew … who it is who says to you, 'Give Me a drink,' you would have asked Him, and He would have given you living water." It was *necessary* for this woman to have a proper understanding of the gift and the giver, before her request for salvation would be answered.[80] Later in John's Gospel the Lord confirmed that those who would not accept His true identity would die in their sins (John 8:24).

It is imperative that we properly communicate the identity of the Saviour. Paul became a Christian when he found out who

---

[80] I do not say a *full* understanding but a *proper* understanding. A person can be saved without understanding how salvation works but they can't be saved if they believe that salvation is by works. Likewise, someone may be saved knowing little about Christ — but they can't be saved while denying His deity or sinless humanity.

Jesus was (Acts 9:1-6) and he began his work for the Lord by preaching "Christ in the synagogues, that He is the Son of God" (Acts 9:20). He continued throughout his ministry constantly emphasising the true identity of Jesus.[81] Never has this been more indispensable to evangelism than in the present time; yet very often Christians assume that people know the truth about who Jesus is and lead straight into an appeal to trust Him.

What are the foundational facts of the gospel? We have seen from Romans 3, that what we needed was someone who could act as our substitute and satisfy divine justice in respect of sin. Human beings stand before God as guilty criminals before a righteous judge, and the sentence for their crimes is a payment they can never make, a punishment they can never exhaust.

Four facts about the Lord confirm Him to be the answer to the need of humanity: His deity, humanity, sacrificial death, and bodily resurrection. These form the core beliefs of the Christian faith and people who deny these truths are not saved.[82] These four truths are linked together in this way:

1. His Deity: *He alone* **could** *make a* **sufficient** *sacrifice.* Because He is an infinite person, He could satisfy the claims of infinite justice on the behalf of a sinful world.

2. His Humanity: *He* **could** *make a* **substitutionary** *sacrifice.* Because He is a real man, yet a holy man, He

---

[81.] cf. Acts 13:33-39; 17:2-3; 28:31; Rom. 1:1-7; 1 Cor. 1:23-24; 2:2; 3:10-11; 15:1-11; 2 Cor. 1:18-20; 4:5-6; Eph. 3:8; 1 Tim. 2:3-7 etc.

[82.] cf. John 8:24; Rom. 3:24; 4:5; 10:9; 1 Cor. 15:1-19; Eph. 2:8-9; 1 John 4:2-3.

could substitute for men – taking their punishment upon Himself.

3. His Death: *He **did** make a **substitutionary** sacrifice.* What He could do by virtue of His humanity, He has done. "Christ ... suffered once for sins, the just for the unjust, that He might bring us to God" (1 Pet. 3:18).

4. His Resurrection: *He **did** make a **sufficient** sacrifice.* What He alone could do by virtue of His deity, He has done. God has confirmed His acceptance of the sufficiency of the death of Christ by His resurrection from the dead.

As these are four essential gospel truths, we must make it our business to instruct people of them.

I remember a conversation with Johnny, who wondered what I meant when I said that we needed someone to pay the price to enable our release from punishment. I used the following analogy:

Suppose you were in court for committing a crime. The evidence is against you, and the verdict is reached – you are guilty. The time comes for sentencing and the judge sentences you to pay a large fine – so large that you know you'll never be able to pay it. If the fine is not paid, you will go to prison. You come out of the court, and sit on a bench with your head in your hands. What can you do? You can't undo the crime you've committed and you can't pay the fine. You are trapped with no way to escape the prison you deserve.

*Just then someone sits down beside you and, looking up,
you are surprised to recognise the face of the judge. He says,
"You did commit the crime, didn't you?" "Yes." "So you do
deserve the punishment?" "Of course," you say, "but I can
never pay that fine!" He looks at you. "In the court I had to
uphold the law, I had to find you guilty, and I had to sentence
you correctly." Then he says, "However, I'm sorry for you."
At this, he reaches into his pocket, and pulls out an envelope
stuffed with money. He says, "I can settle the fine."*

At this point I asked Johnny, "Would you be thankful?" "Of
course," he said, "but who would do something like that?"
"God would!" I said, and took some time to show how this
story illustrates the gospel: "God is the judge, and we are
guilty. He knows what we deserve, and has sentenced us to
a judgment we can never exhaust, a penalty we can never
pay – eternity in hell. This prison looms before us all. Yet,
the Judge loves us and has come to where we are "to save
sinners" (1 Tim. 1:15). He has gone to the cross and willingly
paid the price for our release, satisfying the demands of
justice to provide salvation for us.

Johnny was truly impressed by this. That God would do
such a thing had never occurred to him. He understood for
the first time what the gospel message was. I explained that
justice had been satisfied, and Christ was raised from the
dead as confirmation of this fact.

This simple illustration incorporates teaching concerning
the person and work of the Lord Jesus Christ. It is a simple
explanation of the basic truths of the gospel. It either implies

or directly states the four foundational truths of the gospel message: the deity, humanity, sacrificial death, and bodily resurrection of Christ.

We must emphasise the need for the clear communication of these truths. A century ago in the United Kingdom, and in the Western world, these biblical teachings about the Lord Jesus Christ were more widely known, even if not personally believed. However, they are, at present, usually unknown. The devil has employed many weapons in his arsenal to undermine the basic knowledge of the man on the street about Christ.

Think, for example, of the confusion of the cults. Jehovah's Witnesses distribute a magazine which apparently teaches about Jesus. However, the "Jesus" they present is not the biblical Jesus. Also, some atheists have gone so far as to suggest that the historical "Jesus" never existed. Even though they are flying in the face of all sober historical study, their words have a tremendous impact on their gullible followers. Many recent publications purport to have fresh and alarming insights into the life and death of the Lord; they offer wild speculation and conspiracy theories about Christianity. Then there is the rise of Islam and its recognition of Jesus as a prophet but not as the Son of God or the substitute for men.

Non-Christians are bombarded with confusing and contradictory messages about Christ. Christians gain their knowledge of Him and His work largely from the New Testament, a collection of divinely-inspired books made up of first-century documents written by the apostles and their close companions.[83] Most non-Christians, however, gain their knowledge of Christ from television programs, speculative novels, magazine articles, films, and chat shows. Make no mistake, the "Jesus" presented is not the same. Anyone with even limited knowledge of the Bible can see that many of the common notions about Jesus promoted in society are false representations of the Lord. However, most do not have *any* true Bible knowledge and are open to the education they receive from Google.

It is our responsibility, therefore, to *teach* the gospel; truth must be known before trust can be placed in it. It may not always be possible or necessary to set out detailed or structured arguments for the deity and humanity, death and resurrection of Christ. However, at the very least, we should ensure we announce these truths accurately. We must remember that for a person to be *saved*, they must not have a false understanding of the gospel; these facts form the basis of that message which is "the power of God to salvation for everyone who believes" (Rom. 1:16).

A simple method for instructing others is to weave into your conversation rudimentary truth about the Lord Jesus Christ. Unless you are certain that the unbeliever knows the gospel well, assume that they do not know it at all. Instead of hastily quoting many Bible verses, and bombarding the unbeliever with information, take things slowly and explain as you go. For example, instead of saying simply that "Christ Jesus came into the world to save sinners"

[83.] More on this in chapter 11.

(1 Tim. 1:15), you could expand and explain as you go along: "Christ Jesus [the one who was God and lived in heaven with His Father] came into the world [voluntarily becoming a real man] to save sinners [that means to rescue us from our sins and from hell]." By doing this, you are *teaching*. In this example, the sinner learns that Christ is in nature God, the eternal Son of the Father; she is taught that He came from heaven, that His incarnation was a voluntary act in which He took to Himself true humanity. She also learns that the salvation He came to provide is for her, and has both moral and eternal implications.

If we assume that most people have no true knowledge of the gospel, we will not be far wrong. Joan came to hear the gospel being preached some years ago and has continued to attend gospel meetings. She is an alcoholic, and sincerely desires deliverance. In recent times I started studies through Mark's Gospel with her. I was amazed to learn that she had no idea that the Bible taught that Jesus was God; she had no notion that His death was a part of God's plan. This woman has listened to the gospel being preached well, but she never grasped these essential gospel facts until time was taken to slowly and deliberately *instruct* her. Recognising the wilful resistance of the human mind to divine truth, and the tireless energies of the "god of this age" (2 Cor. 4:4) to blind the unbeliever, we must be willing to take time with people and clearly articulate our message in understandable language, step-by-step, as the person is able to receive it.

It is also essential for us to listen well and pick up any hints that suggest we are not being understood. Sometimes, because of previous influences, people hear what they expect to hear, not what we want them to hear.

Clare, a girl in her twenties, was very willing to chat about spiritual matters. I thought I could go straight to the gospel as her attitude suggested background knowledge. When I mentioned that Jesus Christ was God, she agreed wholeheartedly. However, I soon found out that she thought *I* was god too! In fact, she believed that we were all part of the divine – we had just forgotten it. I had to clarify what I meant by God, explain in what sense Jesus was God, and teach what the Bible meant by man being made in God's image.

You can see that a simple invitation to "receive Christ" would not have been enough for Clare. She needed time spent in explanation; she needed to be taught clearly those facts which we often assume are widely known. She needed to be instructed in what I meant by the terms I used. This is true of many people. We must ensure that they are hearing what we *mean*, not just what we say.

Gospel Compassion

The gospel message concerns the love of God for lost and ruined sinners. This love must be reflected in those who carry it. We "are ambassadors for Christ, as though God were pleading through us" (2 Cor. 5:20). We may speak much of God's compassion, and our own, but our actions will reveal the truth to those around us. True compassion for souls is not something that we simply choose to *show*; it is something that we determine to *have*. If we have it, it will show.

The Lord's sincere spiritual concern for the woman of Samaria, and the Samaritan people, can be easily traced as we read the story. The first evidence of true compassion is that the Lord went to where she was. This was no chance encounter – the Lord had deliberately chosen this route for her blessing. When she arrived, He set aside personal weariness to speak to her. Religious, racial, and social barriers were all crossed as He disregarded cultural norms to make her comfortable enough to engage with Him. In addition, He showed personal interest in her by use of language and analogies which she could understand and by listening to her questions carefully, answering the issues she raised. He raised the sin issue discreetly but without minimising her moral failure. He revealed God as a Father who was seeking for people just like her. Gently and winsomely He led her towards a proper understanding of Himself.

We need to learn to manifest this same compassion. If we have genuine love for souls, it will be seen in:

Our Behaviour

Mahatma Gandhi reportedly said, "I like your Christ, I do not like your Christians. Your Christians are so unlike your Christ."[84] While we may not give Gandhi the credit for truly liking Christ or for being very objective in his criticism, yet we all know that there is some truth expressed by this statement. Because Christianity claims to change how people live, it suffers often through the lives of those who profess it.

---

[84] There is some dispute about the origin of this quotation.

We must determine, as Paul wrote to the Christians at Philippi, to let our "conduct be worthy of the gospel of Christ" (1:27). Every day that we live we are responsible to behave in such a way as commends the gospel. R. C. Chapman was once told that he had no great gift for preaching the gospel; his response was to say, "There are many who preach Christ, but not many who live Christ. My great aim will be to live Christ."[85] As well as being our duty towards God, this is a matter of genuine love for the lost. Peter reminded his readers of the necessity of maintaining honourable conduct "among the Gentiles, that when they speak against you as evildoers, they may, by your good works which they observe, glorify God in the day of visitation" (1 Pet. 2:12). By the conduct of believers, sinners can be prepared to receive the gospel when they hear it. Sadly, the reverse is also true; there is nothing which hinders the gospel as much as the hypocritical lives of professed believers.

Our Friendships
Love will necessarily involve association with sinners. In Mark 2, Levi opened his home to the Lord and, as a result,

> ... as He was dining in Levi's house ... many tax collectors
> and sinners also sat together with Jesus and His disciples;
> for there were many, and they followed Him. And when the
> scribes and Pharisees saw Him eating with the tax collectors

---

[85.] R. C. Chapman, cited in Robert L. Peterson & Alexander Strauch, *Agape Leadership: Lessons in Spiritual Leadership From The Life Of R. C. Chapman*, Lewis & Roth Publishers, 1991, loc. 120.

and sinners, they said to His disciples, "How is it that He eats and drinks with tax collectors and sinners?" When Jesus heard it, He said to them, "Those who are well have no need of a physician, but those who are sick. I did not come to call the righteous, but sinners, to repentance". (vv. 15-17)

This association with "tax collectors and sinners" drew the ire of the Pharisees time and again in the Lord's ministry (cf. Luke 15:1-2).

The Pharisees were separatists. They believed that they should not associate with irreligious or immoral people. However, the Lord Jesus, along with His disciples, acted differently, and the proud religious leaders were not happy; they thought that the only reason for being in the company of irreligious and immoral people was because you were of the same character. What they had long forgotten was *compassion*. Why does a doctor associate with patients? Is it because he is sick? No. The doctor is close to his patients because he has the cure for their sickness.

We are not encouraged to be separatists.[86] "The commandments of God are ... about being merciful and loving to sinners and at the same time living in personal

---

[86] The subject here is evangelism and the need to build relationships with unbelievers to gain their trust and share the gospel with them. There is no doubt that the scriptures forbid us to be "unequally yoked together with unbelievers" (2 Cor. 6:14) which is a different subject altogether. Also, there are occasions when a believer knows that a friendship is influencing them towards sin. In such circumstances the relationship would be better terminated according to Ps. 1:1; Prov. 1:10-16 etc. However, none of this should cloud our vision for evangelism: "we remain in the world, and to cut off all friendships with non-Christians is, in evangelistic terms, disastrous" (Peter Jeffery, *How Shall They Hear?*, Evangelical Press, 1996, p. 76).

holiness and purity".[87] In this, as in all other matters, "the truth is in Jesus" (Eph. 4:21). "We should not shut ourselves up in Christianized communities. Rather we should seek to befriend the ungodly in order to introduce them to our Lord and Savior."[88] We are to deliberately befriend the lost, not because we have the same interests as them, but because we have a sincere love for their souls. Each person is precious to God, and should be precious to us. We might enjoy the company of like-minded believers much more; the conversation of the ungodly may be hard to endure on occasions; however, we have a *duty* to step outside our comfort zone and to get to know our neighbours and colleagues. Let us not forget that the Lord Jesus undoubtedly found heaven more appealing than earth. The holy company and unremitting adoration of celestial realms was certainly more enjoyable than the sinful atmosphere and persistent hatred of earth. Yet He who was "with God" eternally, entered time and "dwelt among us" (John 1:1, 14), and the reason for His coming was our salvation. "Let this mind be in you which was also in Christ Jesus" (Php. 2:5).

As we associate with unconverted people – while maintaining our spiritual walk with the Lord – we will discover a deepening compassion for them, and a sincere desire for their blessing which will lead us to earnest prayer for their souls. Williams comments, "It's hard sometimes to have compassion for huge groups of people that we don't

---

[87] Barrs, *The Heart of Evangelism*, p.147.
[88] William MacDonald, *Believers Bible Commentary*, Thomas Nelson Publishers, 1995.

know from Adam. But if we share our lives with people, if we make genuine friendships with them and pray for them, we will increasingly grow to love them. Then compassion for them will drive us to overcome our fears and tell them about Jesus."[89]

Our Sensitivity

An important chapter about evangelism is found in Paul's first letter to the Christians at Corinth. In a large section of that letter (chapters 6-10), Paul considers the subject of Christian liberty. He bookends the section by making clear that the Christian has no freedom in respect of immorality (chapter 6) or idolatry (chapter 10). However, in chapters 7-9 he shows that there are areas in which the Christian has freedom to make choices. These include the areas of marriage, food, and service.

When dealing with the subject of marriage, Paul shows that each individual should be aware of his own needs. He should know *himself*, and with that knowledge act wisely in his decision whether to marry or not (1 Cor. 7:7-9). In the matter of food, a believer should be sensitive to the conscience of her fellow-believers. She is to take *them* into account, and act wisely (8:9-13).

The subject of evangelism is different however. It is not now self-consideration, or the consideration of other believers which is to the fore; it is the consideration of *sinners*. Paul says:

[89.] Williams, *Intentional*, p. 29.

> *For though I am free from all men, I have made myself a servant*
> *to all, that I might win the more; and to the Jews I became as*
> *a Jew, that I might win Jews; to those who are under the law,*
> *as under the law, that I might win those who are under the*
> *law; to those who are without law, as without law (not being*
> *without law toward God, but under law toward Christ), that I*
> *might win those who are without law; to the weak I became as*
> *weak, that I might win the weak. I have become all things to all*
> *men, that I might by all means save some. Now this I do for the*
> *gospel's sake, that I may be partaker of it with you.* (9:19-23)

Paul became "as a Jew" to win Jews and, he became "as without law" to those without law to win them. Whether among Jews or Gentiles, Paul fitted in, with the purpose of winning them to Christ.

Recently I was speaking to a Christian who said that we must show ourselves to be different *in every way* to the people whom we evangelise; this was how to win them. I pondered over what he said and he was gone before I could reply. However, if this is true, why did the apostle Paul say, "to the Jews I became as a Jew, that I might win Jews" (v. 20)?

Our creed must bend to the Bible and not the Bible to our creed.[90] We should not stop short of what scripture says, nor should we add to it: "Our wisdom is to have our minds open to all scripture, refusing to go a hair-breadth farther".[91]

---

[90] Paraphrased from C. H. Spurgeon, *Spurgeon on Joshua*, Joshua 1:7, Joshua's Obedience, Precept Austin, http://preceptaustin.org/spurgeon_on_joshua.
[91] William Kelly, *Notes on the Epistle to the Romans*, Believers Bookshelf, 1878, reprinted 1978. p. 220.

We are responsible to take into account the unbelievers whom we are evangelising and, if there is something about us likely to hinder their response to our message, we should set it aside.[92] Paul applied this principle. He wanted Timothy to accompany him in evangelism and he "took him and circumcised him because of the Jews who were in that region, for they all knew that his father was Greek" (Acts 16:3). Paul knew the people to whom he was going, and he took them into account, removing perceived hindrances to their reception of the gospel in advance. We should never conform to sinful practices, but neither should we insist upon our personal preferences or extra-biblical traditions.

Paul's words in 1 Corinthians 9 were not placing upon believers another rule but showing what *genuine love* caused him to do. From a cultural perspective, Paul was no longer a Jew, and he was not a Gentile. Yet, he did not view himself as being part of a third culture called "Christian culture" which he should champion. Rather, he found that he could relate to any culture, not by compromising his Christian character or disobeying biblical commands, but by removing unnecessary barriers to reaching sinners, *without compromise.*

This is searching. As Christians, we need to ask ourselves whether we love those around us enough to remove obstacles which divide us from them. Are we willing to order our lives, and set aside our own preferences, so that we can reach them? This is what the Saviour did (John 1:14;

[92.] We are not referring here to Biblical commands but to personal preferences.

Rom. 8:3-4; Php. 2:6-8; Heb. 2:14-18; 4:15), and this is what He calls us to do (John 20:21). Too often we are more concerned about pleasing ourselves, or pleasing other Christians, than we are about reaching the lost with the gospel. It is easy to build up a heritage of traditions that separate us from the very people we are responsible to evangelise. We must, if we are to fulfil our gospel responsibility, be willing to discard extra-biblical traditions, lest they cause us to sin (cf. Mark 7:1-13).[93]

Gospel Choice

Preaching Christ involves setting before each person a choice. Unfortunately, some "treat Christian truth like chewing gum, spending hours chewing it over in discussion, but never swallowing it."[94] We must ensure that each person is made aware of the response they should make to the gospel.

The term "appeal" has fallen on hard times because of its sad misuse; however, there *is* an appeal in the gospel, and this must be communicated. The Lord Jesus, on many memorable occasions, entreated His audience to trust Him. While the provision of salvation is God's responsibility alone, the reception of salvation involves a choice by the sinner.

In John 4, the invitation of the Lord was implied rather than direct. "If you knew ... you would have asked Him" (v. 10) and "whoever drinks of the water that I shall give him

---

[93.] Biblical *truth* should never be discarded no matter the circumstance. However we should be willing, if circumstances demand, to discard any *tradition* which is not found in God's word.

[94.] Kenneth Prior, *The Gospel in a Pagan Society*, Christian Focus Publications, 1995, p. 97

will never thirst" (v. 14). The choice to be made was both informed and personal. She must have information before she could make it, and she must personally appropriate the blessing available to her.

As to the importance of making an *informed* choice, we need to be wary of the fact that multitudes have professed faith in Christ and have shown no evidence of true conversion. One reason for this is that people have no idea why they are "trusting" or whom they are "trusting". We have already emphasised that a proper understanding of what the gift is, and who the giver is, is necessary for salvation.

By using the analogy of drinking, the Lord stresses that this informed choice is a very *personal* one. No one can drink for you. Notice the responsibility of each sinner, the availability of salvation, and the certainty of blessing for all who believe.

Responsibility

Words such as "ask" (v. 10) and "drink" (v.14) imply an exercise of the person's own will. To request or receive something involves a choice being made. Examining the life of the Lord Jesus, we can see that He firmly placed the responsibility for personal blessing on the shoulders of the sinner.

The Lord communicated the need for sinners to repent, believe, come, follow, seek, receive, ask, drink, eat, and enter in. Many of these words were later used by the apostles, along with additions exhorting sinners to obey, accept, confess, call, or take. These appeals demand a decision; they place responsibility on the recipient of the gospel message.

Everywhere in scripture, men and women are treated as responsible beings who are faced with a choice as to their relationship with God. Among all God's creatures, man is unique, being made in the image of God. One result of this is that man has the ability to make his own choices.[95] At creation, the repeated refrain "God said"[96] was the only prerequisite to the fulfilment of God's will: "He spoke, and it was done; He commanded, and it stood fast" (Ps. 33:9). However, in Genesis 2, God spoke again to man and it is important to see how He worded His command: "Of every tree of the garden you may freely eat; but of the tree of the knowledge of good and evil you shall not eat, for in the day that you eat of it you shall surely die" (Gen. 2:16-17). God presented to man an *option*. He said in effect — *you have a choice, and there will be consequences.*

God, as the sovereign creator of the universe, has given to man tremendous freedom. A. W Tozer has put it like this:

> *Here is my view: God sovereignly decreed that man should be free to exercise moral choice, and man from the beginning has fulfilled that decree by making choice between good and evil ... If in His absolute freedom God has willed to give man limited freedom, who is there to stay His hand or say, "What doest thou?" Man's will is free because God is sovereign.*[97]

[95.] His choices are self-determined. The source of a man's choices is his own will.

[96.] See Gen. 1:3, 6, 9, 11, 14, 20, 24, 26, 28, 29; 2:18.

[97.] A. W. Tozer, *The Knowledge of the Holy*, Authentic Media, 2008, pp. 144-5.

Man, therefore, can make free choices – choices for which God will hold him accountable.[98] This was true from the beginning, and has never ceased to be the case.

While the human family has been severely damaged by Adam's fall, yet *man has not ceased to be man*. The distinctive features which marked him out from the beginning remain. Human beings are still in the "image of God" (Gen. 1:27; 9:6), and have not become the equivalent of animals or robots; our choices are not determined *for* us, but *by* us.

Because this is the case, we must not fail to faithfully present to each person their responsibility before God. A good gospel conversation will leave a person conscious of their responsibility to repent and believe the gospel. Paul consistently preached "repentance toward God and faith toward our Lord Jesus Christ" (Acts 20:21).

We are "ambassadors for Christ, as though God were pleading through us". We are to "implore … on Christ's behalf" that sinners "be reconciled to God" (2 Cor. 5:20). God is appealing, beseeching, entreating sinners. If this was not recorded in scripture we would not have dared to say it. However, it *is* recorded. We stand as the representatives of Christ and we implore, we beseech sinners to be reconciled to God.

[98.] When I speak of free choices I am not saying that man is free from divine *influence*. I am saying that man makes choices free from divine *determination*. Divine influence is brought to bear upon men or they never would be saved. However, when a human being makes a choice, it is made *by* him, not *for* him. To put it simply: each person could respond to God in other ways than he does respond.

Availability

The gospel offer is genuine. The appeals of God toward sinners have a purpose: God our Saviour "desires all men to be saved and to come to the knowledge of the truth" (1 Tim. 2:4). He "did not send His Son into the world to condemn the world, but that the world through Him might be saved" (John 3:17).

We are not restricted in our offer of the gospel. The Lord managed, in the few words of invitation that He made, to communicate to the woman that salvation was available *for her*. "If you knew the gift of God, and who it is who says to you, 'Give Me a drink,' you would have asked Him, and He would have given you living water." (John 4:10). This is because, as He later affirmed, "*whoever* drinks of the water that I shall give him will never thirst" (v. 14, emphasis added).

Man has a real, and very solemn, choice to make because God "commands all men everywhere to repent" (Acts 17:30), and the gospel invitation promises blessing to "whoever believes" (John 3:15-16; 11:26; 12:46; Acts 10:43; Rom. 9:33; 10:11; 1 John 5:1), "whoever drinks" (John 4:14), and "whoever calls" (Acts 2:21; Rom. 10:13). The final great gospel invitation of scripture should be *our* appeal to sinners: "Whoever desires, let him take the water of life freely" (Rev. 22:17).

If salvation was not available for all then we could not "on Christ's behalf" (2 Cor. 5:20) make a genuine appeal to each person we meet.

What means a universal call
If there be not enough for all?[99]

God is "not willing that any should perish but that all should come to repentance" (2 Pet. 3:9). So, with clear conscience, with honest desire, with urgent pleadings, we can call upon sinners to repent: to acknowledge before God their sinfulness and helplessness, and to receive Jesus Christ as their Lord and Saviour (Rom. 10:9; Acts 16:31).

Certainty

The Lord Jesus Christ added assurances to his appeals. In response to her asking, He would "have given ... living water" (John 4:10). Salvation would be granted. And, to the person who appropriates salvation, the promise is that he "will never thirst. But the water that I shall give him will become in him a fountain of water springing up into everlasting life" (v.14).

No one needs to fear that faith in Christ will not result in salvation, or that salvation will be a disappointment. "Come to Me ... I *will* give you rest" (Matt. 11:28, emphasis added), and "the one who comes to Me I will by no means cast out" (John 6:37). Each sinner can be assured that trusting Christ brings certain salvation, spiritual satisfaction, and eternal security.

Paul had complete confidence in his message. He knew that the "gospel of Christ ... is the power of God to

---

[99] William Blane, 'The Atonement', *Lays of Life and Hope*, John Ritchie Ltd, 1991, pp. 12-13.

salvation for everyone who believes" (Rom. 1:16). We can have that same confidence, and we should convey this assurance to others. Almost two millennia have passed since Paul preached the gospel, and every person who has since trusted the risen Christ to save them has experienced God's power in their deliverance.

Never forget that evangelism is *telling sinners the gospel so that they may be saved*. "The great practical end of the gospel is to bring the human heart into obedience to Christ and to make the stubborn will acknowledge allegiance to His sway".[100] We must not neglect to urge the sinner to repent and believe in the Lord.

A Gospel Summary

As a young Christian, I attempted to create a succinct summary of the gospel for use in situations in which I had only one minute or so to communicate the salient points. When someone appeared reluctant to get into a lengthy conversation, I would ask: "Do you know the gospel?" and when they said, "No," I'd continue, "Well, if you give me just one minute of your time, I can share it with you." I then shared a concise, memorised gospel message.[101] The following is an example of a summary which contains the necessary ingredients of the gospel, yet can be communicated in just over one minute:

---

[100] C. H. Spurgeon, cited in Stephen McCaskell (compiler), *Through the Eyes of C. H. Spurgeon: Quotes from a Reformed Baptist Pastor*, 2012, p. 85.

[101] I am not suggesting that this is the best approach to sharing the gospel. Rather, in non-ideal circumstances, it is good to be able to tell people briefly and accurately what it is you believe. Also, if called upon to *publicly* state your beliefs, such a memorised summary will cut out a lot of waffle and enable you to speak with confidence.

The Christian gospel states that God is the Creator of the universe and we are accountable to Him for how we live. In God's view, every one of us is the same — we have rebelled against His authority and broken His laws — we all deserve His judgment in hell. However, God loved us so much that He sent His Son to be our Saviour. He who was God became man and, upon the cross, took the punishment for sin, making full payment for our salvation. God raised His Son from the dead to show that all the work required for our salvation was done. Because of what Jesus Christ has done, salvation is provided for you! However, if you want to be saved, you need to own up to your sin, turn to God, and trust Christ alone to save you. God promises that if you believe on the Lord Jesus Christ you will be saved from hell and sure of heaven.

After concluding, it is always good to ask a question such as: "Have you ever heard that before?" or, "What would your thoughts be on that?" or, "Does that make sense to you?" A concise presentation of the gospel message can sometimes reopen the conversation, affording an opportunity to give further explanation.

We recommend that you have your own crisp outline of gospel truth committed to memory for those occasions in which a brief opportunity is given. A similarly-crafted personal testimony will also be very helpful for those unexpected opportunities God will open for you.

The Gospel is a fact; therefore tell it simply. The Gospel is a joyful fact; therefore tell it cheerfully. The Gospel is an entrusted fact; therefore tell it faithfully. The Gospel is a fact of infinite moment; therefore tell it earnestly. The Gospel is a fact of infinite love; therefore tell it feelingly. The Gospel is a fact of difficult comprehension to many; therefore tell it with illustration. The Gospel is a fact about a Person; therefore preach Christ.[102]

[102.] Archibald Brown, cited in Leonard Ravenhill, *Why Revival Tarries*, Bethany House Publishers, 1987, p. 64.

Part Two:
Apologetics

Chapter 6

AN APOLOGETIC FOR APOLOGETICS

*But even if you should suffer for righteousness' sake, you
will be blessed. Have no fear of them, nor be troubled, but
in your hearts honor Christ the Lord as holy, always being
prepared to make a defense to anyone who asks you for a
reason for the hope that is in you; yet do it with gentleness
and respect, having a good conscience, so that, when you
are slandered, those who revile your good behavior in
Christ may be put to shame.* 1 Peter 3:14-16, ESV

It was an opportunity that any evangelist would love to have.
We got a phone call from a woman who wanted us to visit her
because she was interested in knowing more about God. She
welcomed us into her house and as we were heading towards
the sitting room she started pouring out her questions.

"Right," she said, "I've got loads of questions. Has the
Bible not been changed and corrupted? Has science not

proven that we evolved from monkeys? Why would God allow all the evil and suffering in the world? What about all the other religions? Why do I need Jesus?"

How would you have responded to a barrage of questions like that? I imagine they are questions you have heard before, and probably wondered about yourself, but have you ever taken time to get answers?

In the time it took for us to walk from her front door to her sitting room she raised pretty much all the objections you are ever going to face in evangelism. Look at the subjects of her questions: scripture, science, suffering, salvation and the Saviour. Almost any objection an unbeliever will raise will fall into one of those categories. So if you have thought through these issues you will be able to present a positive case for the gospel whenever you encounter an objection. That's the purpose of this second section of the book. It was very worthwhile in the case of this woman, because a few days after our conversation, she trusted Christ to save her.[103]

When Peter tells us in 1 Peter 3:15 that we are to be ready to give an answer (or a defence), he uses the Greek word from which we get the word *apologetics*. Even though there is this command to give an apologetic for our hope, many Christians are sceptical about the whole enterprise. They think we are being unfaithful to God and undermining His authority when we present arguments and evidence for the truth of His word – we should just assert it instead, and if

---

[103.] Needless to say, the Lord had been working in her heart and we were just one link in the chain, but she had questions that were standing in the way of her coming to Christ, and they needed to be addressed.

someone doesn't accept the authority of the Bible then we have no message for them. Also, they believe it is unfruitful to try to reason with people about these issues – it just doesn't work – "You can't argue someone into the Kingdom." Let's think about these statements and see if there's anything to them, because we certainly don't want to dishonour God by being unfaithful to scripture, and neither do we want to waste our time by doing anything unfruitful.

Is it unfaithful to scripture?[104]

The Bible is full of apologetics. In fact, the greatest apologist of all is the Triune God.

God gave evidence

When God caught Moses' attention at the burning bush (Ex. 3) and commissioned him to go to Egypt and deliver His message to the children of Israel, He didn't merely give Moses the gist of what to say; four times over He gave him the exact words: "Thus you shall say to the children of Israel ..." (see Ex. 3:14, 15, 16, 18). So Moses was going to the Israelites with the very words of God, in all their power, with all their authority, carrying all their weight. But then Moses asked God what would happen if the Israelites didn't believe (4:1). How did God respond to that question? He gave Moses three miraculous signs to perform as proof that he was indeed speaking from and for God.

This is how God always operated when giving new

[104.] As we delve into each subject in the subsequent chapters we will draw on many scripture references.

revelation. He never expected or asked people just to believe based on the word of the prophet. The prophets didn't merely say they had a message from God, they showed it. They always gave evidence that they were speaking with divine authority, whether that took the form of miracles or predictive prophecy; there was something tangible and testable to validate their claim to be God's channels of revelation.

Think of how He participated in the contest Elijah set up at Mount Carmel in 1 Kings 18. He didn't feel insulted or demeaned that the people weren't persuaded solely by the authority of His word. He was prepared to provide evidence that He was the true God in contrast to Baal, so He did something that only an omnipotent being could do.

In Isaiah 41, God Himself challenges the false gods to provide some evidence of their reality. Listen to what He says:

> *Produce your cause, saith the LORD; bring forth your strong reasons, saith the King of Jacob. Let them bring them forth, and show us what shall happen: let them show the former things, what they be, that we may consider them, and know the latter end of them; or declare us things for to come. Show the things that are to come hereafter, that we may know that ye are gods: yea, do good, or do evil, that we may be dismayed, and behold it together.* (Isa. 41:21-23, KJV)

The fulfilment of prophecy is cited here as evidence for Yahweh being the true God. He did something that only an omniscient being could do to prove that He had spoken.

Christ gave evidence

It was said of the Lord Jesus that no one ever spoke like Him (John 7:46). His word had power and His teaching had authority that struck people and stuck with them (Luke 4:32). Even though His words were so compelling, and every single syllable He uttered came with all the authority of God Himself, He was still prepared to provide additional proof that He was who He claimed to be and His words were the words of God.

Look at what happened in Mark 2:5-12:

When Jesus saw their faith, He said to the paralytic, "Son, your sins are forgiven you."

And some of the scribes were sitting there and reasoning in their hearts, "Why does this Man speak blasphemies like this? Who can forgive sins but God alone?"

But immediately, when Jesus perceived in His spirit that they reasoned thus within themselves, He said to them, "Why do you reason about these things in your hearts? Which is easier, to say to the paralytic, 'Your sins are forgiven you,' or to say, 'Arise, take up your bed and walk'? But that you may know that the Son of Man has power on earth to forgive sins"— He said to the paralytic, "I say to you, arise, take up your bed, and go to your house." Immediately he arose, took up the bed, and went out in the presence of them all, so that all were amazed and glorified God, saying, "We never saw anything like this!"

This paralysed man was lowered to the feet of the Lord Jesus Christ, and the Lord looked beyond a body stricken by paralysis to a soul stained by sin. He knew that the man's paralysed body wouldn't condemn him to hell, but his sin-stained past would, so the Lord met the man's major need first by forgiving his sins.

The scribes sitting under the sound of His voice were shocked. *Who does He think He is? Only God can forgive sins!* The Lord Jesus knew what they were thinking, so He did something that would testify to His divine power and thus give proof of His divine authority.

This is similar to what He said in John 14:11:

Believe Me that I am in the Father and the Father in Me, or else believe Me for the sake of the works themselves.

The Lord didn't just assert His essential unity with the Father; He pointed to His miracles to confirm His claim. He didn't insist they believe His words just because His words are authoritative and self-authenticating (which of course they are). He graciously provided evidence that His words can be trusted.

That same night in the upper room, the Lord gave His disciples a lot of information about things that lay ahead of them. Look at what He said after He told them about the treachery of Judas:

Now I tell you before it comes, that when it does come to pass, you may believe that I am He. (John 13:19)

Then He told them that He was going away. In John 14:29 He said:

And now I have told you before it comes, that when it does come to pass, you may believe.

The Lord knew that there were clouds on the horizon that were going to burst upon these disciples. In the storm that they were going to brave, He wanted them to have complete confidence in Him and His word. Therefore He gave them objective evidence of His deity and trustworthiness.

Tying this together, we see that the Lord Jesus used the two evidences God used in the Old Testament to give proof that He was indeed who He claimed to be and that His words were authoritative: miracles and prophecy. The apostles pointed to these same two proofs that Jesus of Nazareth was indeed the promised Messiah.[105]

The Holy Spirit gave evidence

When the Lord sent His disciples out to preach the gospel, He assured them they weren't going in their own power – the Holy Spirit of God Himself was going to indwell and empower them. These apostles were invested with unique authority and were the communicators of new revelation from God. The truth they taught is now our New Testament. Does that mean then that all they did was proclaim the

---

[105.] Miracles – Acts 2:22; 10:38. They focussed particularly on the supreme miracle of the resurrection – Acts 2:24; 3:15; 10:41; 13:30; 17:31, etc. Fulfilled prophecy – Acts 2:25-36; 3:17-18; 10:43; 13:27-37; 17:1-3, etc.

truth God had revealed to them? No, as we have seen, they pointed to miracles and fulfilled prophecy in relation to Christ as evidence, but there was more:

> *Therefore we must give the more earnest heed to the things we have heard, lest we drift away. For if the word spoken through angels proved steadfast, and every transgression and disobedience received a just reward, how shall we escape if we neglect so great a salvation, which at the first began to be spoken by the Lord, and was confirmed to us by those who heard Him, God also bearing witness both with signs and wonders, with various miracles, and gifts of the Holy Spirit, according to His own will?* (Heb. 2:1-4)

Imagine the situation of a first-century Jew. He was in the only God-given religion. A major feature of that religion was the ceremonial aspect of it. There were sacrifices and offerings, feasts and fasts, rituals and ordinances. Then these disciples of the crucified Nazarene came along preaching that such things were now redundant and finished. What they were saying carried divine authority and came with divine power, but the Holy Spirit carried out mighty signs to authenticate the message they preached. He also gave people the gift of predictive prophecy to mark them out as bona fide prophets (e.g. Acts 11:28). These channels of divine revelation were marked out as such by evidential and miraculous means.

If God (Father, Son and Holy Spirit), was willing to give evidence for His own revelation to mankind, then we should be too.

Not with wisdom of words?

But what about Paul's words in 1 Corinthians 1 and 2? Is he not dismissive of the idea of reasoning with someone about the gospel? Look at what he said:

> For Christ did not send me to baptize, but to preach the gospel, not with wisdom of words, lest the cross of Christ should be made of no effect.

> For the message of the cross is foolishness to those who are perishing, but to us who are being saved it is the power of God. For it is written:

> > "I will destroy the wisdom of the wise,
> > And bring to nothing the understanding of the prudent."

> Where is the wise? Where is the scribe? Where is the disputer of this age? Has not God made foolish the wisdom of this world? For since, in the wisdom of God, the world through wisdom did not know God, it pleased God through the foolishness of the message preached to save those who believe. For Jews request a sign, and Greeks seek after wisdom; but we preach Christ crucified, to the Jews a stumbling block and to the Greeks foolishness, but to those who are called, both Jews and Greeks, Christ the power of God and the wisdom of God. Because the foolishness of God is wiser than men, and the weakness of God is stronger than men.

For you see your calling, brethren, that not many wise according to the flesh, not many mighty, not many noble, are called. But God has chosen the foolish things of the world to put to shame the wise, and God has chosen the weak things of the world to put to shame the things which are mighty; and the base things of the world and the things which are despised God has chosen, and the things which are not, to bring to nothing the things that are, that no flesh should glory in His presence. (1 Cor. 1:17-29)

And I, brethren, when I came to you, did not come with excellence of speech or of wisdom declaring to you the testimony of God. For I determined not to know anything among you except Jesus Christ and Him crucified. I was with you in weakness, in fear, and in much trembling. And my speech and my preaching were not with persuasive words of human wisdom, but in demonstration of the Spirit and of power, that your faith should not be in the wisdom of men but in the power of God. (1 Cor. 2:1-5)

Is Paul saying we shouldn't try to reason with people, give them evidence, or show them proof? Is his point that we just preach the gospel and never deal with people's objections? I don't think so. Here are a few reasons why.

First, it would completely contradict Luke's account of Paul's approach at Corinth:

And he reasoned in the synagogue every Sabbath, and persuaded both Jews and Greeks. (Acts 18:4)

Paul went to the synagogue in Corinth and *reasoned* and *persuaded*. The idea of *reasoning* is disputing/discussing/debating. It is a word that is frequently used of Paul's evangelistic approach.[106] He did not just assert that what he said was true, he backed it up with evidence and answered objections to his position.

Secondly, it would contradict the account he gave of his own preaching at Corinth.

Moreover, brethren, I declare to you the gospel which I preached to you, which also you received and in which you stand, by which also you are saved, if you hold fast that word which I preached to you—unless you believed in vain.

For I delivered to you first of all that which I also received: that Christ died for our sins according to the Scriptures, and that He was buried, and that He rose again the third day according to the Scriptures, and that He was seen by Cephas, then by the twelve. After that He was seen by over five hundred brethren at once, of whom the greater part remain to the present, but some have fallen asleep. After that He was seen by James, then by all the apostles. Then last of all He was seen by me also, as by one born out of due time. (1 Cor. 15:1-8)

Paul, an apostle with divinely-given authority and direct revelations from God, did not just preach, "Christ died for our sins and was buried and was raised." He gave evidence,

---

[106.] e.g. Acts 17:2, 17; 18:19; 19:8, 9; 24:25.

based on fulfilled prophecy and eyewitness testimony, to the reality and reliability of the message he preached. Whatever Paul meant in 1 Corinthians 1 and 2, he certainly did not mean that we should not use reason or provide evidence in our presentation of the gospel.

> *Those who denigrate philosophy or apologetics based on 1 Corinthians 1-2 need to keep reading to the end of the book! In 1 Corinthians 15, Paul lists the eyewitnesses to the bodily resurrection of Jesus and even tells his readers that most of the five hundred believers who saw Jesus after his resurrection were still alive to be questioned. Paul's emphasis on the foolishness of the cross does not oppose objective evidence and fair-minded investigation.*[107]

Thirdly, it is only on a superficial reading of the verses that we would conclude that Paul was against the use of reason and evidence. A careful and correct reading of the passages in question will show us that what Paul was against was altering his message to suit the tastes of his audience. He didn't disguise the message as something it wasn't. The idea of a crucified Messiah was something repulsive to a Jew and ridiculous to a Greek, but Paul didn't try to sand the rough edges off the old rugged cross; he didn't put an appealing veil of sophistication over it. As Harry Ironside said, "He realized it was quite possible by the flowers of rhetoric to cover up, to

---

[107.] Paul Copan & Kenneth D. Litwak, *The Gospel in the Marketplace of Ideas: Paul's Mars Hill Experience for Our Pluralistic World*, IVP, 2014, p. 22.

obscure the shame of the cross".[108] This was the foundation and focus of the message, and he shone the spotlight directly on it. Paul wasn't interested in wooing an audience and winning admiration through oratory that would appeal to Corinthian culture. He didn't want a following for himself or people latching on to him because he used the biggest words and had the best presentation. He wanted people to grasp the significance of the cross. What passed for "excellency of speech" and "wisdom" in Corinth would hinder people getting the message; drawing attention to the evidence certainly wouldn't.

So the Triune God always gave evidence that He had spoken. By miracles and prophecy He demonstrated the reality of His self-revelation. He never demanded that people just believe. Therefore, when we present evidence, we are following the best possible example.

Is it unfruitful in salvation?

"People are won by the gospel, not by arguments." "It takes the Spirit of God, not our arguments, to change people's hearts."

These statements are true, but what is implied by them (i.e. that arguments have no value, or that the Spirit of God doesn't use arguments) is not. There is no dispute that people are won to Christ through the gospel presented in the power of the Spirit, but the issue is that, like that woman mentioned at the start of this chapter, there are

---

[108.] H. A. Ironside, *1 Corinthians*, Loizeaux Brothers, 1975, p. 80.

often barriers that prevent people giving the gospel a hearing. We have to do what we can to clear away those barriers. People aren't saved through an argument, but they aren't saved through our kindness either, yet no one denies the importance of Christians being kind to the lost. We recognise that a winsome Christian character will remove emotional barriers and attract people to hear the gospel. Using apologetics does exactly the same job in the intellectual sphere: it removes the intellectual barriers that the world and the devil have constructed to block a sinner's path to Christ. So defending the faith is a means to an end, not an end in itself.

> *Trusting the mind and using God is tantamount to idolatry; trusting God and using the mind is Christian. Once we get this clear we can see that our intellect is no different from our other talents. It is a gift of God to be used in his service with his help, and not to be trusted as an idol or God-substitute.*[109]

When someone questions the effectiveness of apologetics, we have to ask what he thinks the intended result is. If you measure effectiveness by how many people are saved as a result of a discussion, then you will conclude that using apologetics is not effective, but that is not what apologetic arguments are for. We are not suggesting that presenting apologetics is an alternative to preaching the gospel, just as no one is suggesting that loving people is an alternative

---

[109] John C. Lennox, *Determined to Believe? The Sovereignty of God, Freedom, Faith, and Human Responsibility*, Lion Hudson IP Ltd, 2017, p. 234.

to the gospel. We are suggesting that the use of apologetics achieves different goals that are of great service in the spread of the gospel. For example, being able to give evidence for what you believe has the following benefits:

- It enlarges the believer's appreciation of God's sovereignty over the universe. All truth is God's truth. Every fact in the universe belongs to Him, and it is tremendously encouraging to see how all areas of knowledge rest on one foundation and point in one direction – the God of scripture.

- It stabilises believers. Sometimes even the godliest Christian can be led into circumstances which cause him to doubt. Having objective evidence that doesn't change with changing circumstances can steady him when his subjective experience isn't what it once was or normally is. The well-informed mind can take the shaky emotions by the hand and steady them in times of crisis.

- It equips and encourages believers to reach out with the gospel and converse with people who have a completely different worldview. While we know that the gospel is true from the witness of the Holy Spirit, showing the gospel to be true is another matter, and having answers for the questions you will be asked is a great asset.

- It keeps a conversation going when it might otherwise have shut down. People have questions, and if you aren't prepared to engage with them on those questions then they won't be prepared to listen to what you have to say. We have often spoken to people who started the conversation completely dismissive of anything to do with God, and ended the conversation listening to the gospel and even asking questions about salvation.

- It strips people of the veneer of intellectual justification for their scepticism and exposes the wilful nature of their unbelief. Many in society have been poisoned by atheistic or relativistic viruses that have resulted in them thinking that they have good reasons for rejecting the gospel. By addressing these issues, they are confronted with the truth they have been suppressing, and they are faced with the reality that they have no rational reason for their rebellion.

More could be added, but hopefully you can see that using apologetics is something that encourages strong faith, and it also encourages shared faith.

If they hear not Moses and the prophets ...
However, some have questioned its value based on the dialogue between the rich man and Abraham in Luke 16:

> Then he said, I pray thee therefore, father, that thou wouldest send him to my father's house: for I have five brethren; that he may testify unto them, lest they also come into this place of torment.

Abraham saith unto him, They have Moses and the prophets;
let them hear them.

And he said, Nay, father Abraham: but if one went unto them
from the dead, they will repent.

And he said unto him, If they hear not Moses and the prophets,
neither will they be persuaded, though one rose from the dead.
(vv. 27-31, KJV)

The point that some readers get from this passage is that people aren't convinced or converted by the miraculous, and we should just present God's word to them; if they don't believe God's word then we can and should go no further with them. If this is what the passage teaches then it creates a conflict because, as we have seen, the Triune God gave miraculous evidence to prove that He had spoken. Moreover, the apostles of the Lord also pointed to the historical evidence of the resurrection of Christ in their proclamation of the gospel. It is clear that they didn't take this passage as belittling the importance of the miraculous or as a prohibition on presenting evidence of the miraculous. What then is the point of the passage? Remember the purpose for miracles, and then you will see why they weren't appropriate in this case.

God gave miracles to confirm new revelation and to mark out people as having divinely-given authority. Sending Lazarus to the rich man's brothers does not fit within that paradigm. God had given His word, it had already been attested to, and the brothers presumably already believed it to be God's word. They believed that Moses had received the law of God; they believed the prophets weren't exaggerating when they said "Thus saith the Lord..." It's not that they didn't *believe* Moses and the prophets; it is that they didn't *heed* them. The need these brothers had was to own the seriousness of their guilt and repent. Lazarus coming back from the dead would only confirm the reality of the afterlife, which was something they already believed. It was not the case, then, that these people needed to be convinced in their mind, but rather that they needed to be convicted in their conscience, and a miracle wouldn't do that.

Abraham persisted in his refusal to send Lazarus to warn his brothers, and it is instructive to notice why. It was not that Abraham, or God either, was determined to give people no more than the minimum of evidence. If seeing and hearing an apparition would have brought the brothers to repentance, every room they sat in, every street they walked down, would have been alive with apparitions. But apparitions would not have helped them. They did not need to be convinced that the afterlife is real, or that after death there comes the judgment, or that there is a hell. They needed convinced that their neglect of God's law was serious enough to land them personally in hell. And that was a moral issue, and ultimately a question of God's moral character. The highest possible evidence in the matter therefore was the plain statement of His Word directed to the brothers' moral conscience and judgment. And so it is with us. If our moral judgment is so irresponsible that it can make light of the Bible's warnings of

our guilt before God (see John 3:18; Rom. 1:18, 20; 2:1-3:20),
no amount of seeing of apparitions would convince us that we
personally were in danger of perdition unless we repented.[110]

Are we engaging in a fruitless enterprise when we study and present the evidence for the Christian message? Not at all. In scripture and throughout history many have been saved after being confronted with evidence. It is a tremendously useful tool that the Lord often uses to build up believers, break down barriers, open doors, and prepare hearts for the gospel, all of which is extremely valuable.

Warning

That said, please keep the following warnings from 1 Peter 3:14-16 in mind:

The first is: don't be *distracted*. Our goal in talking to people is not to beat them in an argument but to move them towards Christ. We are to set Christ apart as Lord in our hearts – our aim is not to show how wonderful we are, but how wonderful Christ is. It's possible to have your head full of facts but your heart empty of feeling. You can come away from a conversation saying, "I answered all those objections and he had no answer for my points – I won!" but we aren't in a competition. The person before you isn't a debate opponent, but a perishing soul. Don't be distracted.

Here is a second pitfall to avoid: don't be *dismissive*. When you encounter an objection, don't act like it's stupid.

[110.] D. W. Gooding, *According to Luke*, IVP, 1987, p. 276-277.

Have sympathy with the person. Be understanding of their point of view. If you have wondered about that question tell them that. Don't try to make them look or feel silly. We are to give our answers with gentleness and respect.

Thirdly, don't be *discouraged*. There are two ways in which we can be discouraged: number one is *in light of the responsibility we have* and number two is *in light of the response we get*. We are not responsible to be ready to give an answer to everyone that asks you *any question* – if that were our responsibility then it would be overwhelming. You do not need to know all about physics, biology, psychology, textual criticism, world religions and ancient history to fulfil 1 Peter 3:15. You have to be ready to give an answer to everyone who asks you *for a reason for the hope you have* – you have to be ready with a positive case. That's what we want to help you with in this second section. We hope to show you that these areas where you will be challenged allow you opportunity to present evidence for your faith. You may not know the answers to all their questions, but if you have a reason for your hope then it shows them (and assures you) that there must be answers to their questions. Also, don't be discouraged by the response you get. They may not fall on their knees in repentance when you present the proof of the resurrection. They may not even acknowledge that you made a valid point. As verse 16 says, they may still speak against you. That doesn't mean you haven't done a good job or made a good case. Your responsibility is to present the truth, not to make them accept it.

Fourthly, don't be *disconnected*. The word translated "reason" in verse 15 is *logos*. It's the word we find in John 1:1, "In the beginning was *the Word* ..." John is telling us there that Christ is the one who expresses all that God is, but John 1:14 tells us that the Word was translated into our language: "The Word became flesh ..." God wanted to communicate to mankind, and He did so, clearly and in our language. People got the message. That doesn't mean they received it, but in Christ they got the full revelation of what God is like. So when you give a reason, make sure you communicate clearly. Don't talk over people's heads or in words they don't understand. Don't start lecturing them on some in-depth subject you've just studied. We need to ensure that we are making contact with the person before us.

Conclusion

Secularism and scepticism have elbowed Christian presuppositions out of the public square. They have pushed them out of universities, barred them from the corridors of political power, and ridiculed them in the mainstream media. This means that to reach people with the gospel we have to reach further than once we did. Preaching in Jerusalem to the Pharisees required one approach; preaching in Athens to the philosophers required another. Our culture is, generally speaking, more like Athens than Jerusalem. The people we are called to evangelise don't share our presuppositions, so there will be challenging questions and plenty of objections, and that is scary. Fear is a paralysing emotion, and the fear of getting asked a hard question by an unbeliever keeps many Christians from getting involved in evangelism, and robs them of the joy of spreading the gospel.

One fearful Christian said to us, "But you can't anticipate every question you are going to be asked." That is literally true, but practically false. In practice, you can fairly well anticipate the objections you will get. It is rare that we hear an objection we have never heard before. The lady we mentioned at the start of this chapter raised the five areas from which challenges will arise:

- Scripture – "The Bible is unreliable mythology or irrelevant history."

- Science – "Scientific discovery has disproved the Bible and made God redundant."

- Suffering – "Evil and suffering disprove the existence of a good and powerful God."

- Salvation – "It's narrow minded to say that one way is the only way."

- The Saviour – "Jesus was just a man (if He ever existed at all)."

In the following chapters we will look at these subjects and see that we do not need to fear them. If you get equipped with answers then you can use these challenges to close the gap, remove the obstacles, and not only defend the gospel but advance it as well.

Chapter 7

SCRIPTURE

You are telling me to trust what a book says, but what if it's wrong? I'll be throwing my life away for nothing.

How would you have responded to this remark? Often the response the Christian will give is, "You just have to have faith." Unfortunately, this just reinforces a pervasive and perverted view of faith, which is that faith is just believing something without evidence. If our faith in God's word doesn't have any good reasons supporting it then it isn't a faith that honours God. The following illustration makes the point:

> [S]uppose you meet a man on the street whom you do not recognize, and he gives you a bag with $50,000 in cash and asks you to deposit it in the bank for him. He says that his account number is in the bag. You are surprised because you do not know him at all. You ask, "Why do you trust me with this?" Suppose he says, "No reason; I'm just taking a risk."

What is the effect of that faith in you? Does it honor you? No, it does not. It shows the man is a fool.

But suppose he said, "I know that you don't know me, but I work in the same building you do, and I have watched you for the last year. I have seen your integrity in a dozen ways. I have spoken to people who know you. The reason I am trusting you with this money is that I have good reason to believe you are honest and reliable." Now, what is the effect of that faith? It truly honors you. Why? Because it is based on real evidence that you are honorable. The fruit of such faith is not folly. The fruit of such faith is wisdom, and that faith and wisdom honor the person who is trusted.[111]

There are several ways we can demonstrate that the Bible is God's word,[112] but we will deal with two that we have found easy and effective to use:

1. The prophecies of the Bible
2. The power of the Bible

These two subjects can be quickly presented and readily understood.

---

[111] John Piper, *A Peculiar Glory: How the Christian Scriptures reveal their complete truthfulness*, IVP, 2016, p. 134.

[112] For a more detailed look at the two proofs offered here, and for additional proofs, see Paul McCauley, *Prove It, How you can know and show that the Bible is God's word*, Decapolis Press, 2017.

1. The prophecies of the Bible

The Bible stands apart from all the so-called holy books of world religions in that the Bible alone explicitly deals with prophecy.[113] There are prophecies relating to the nation of Israel, the Gentile nations, and the coming Messiah. The prophecies relating to the Gentile nations and to Israel have not played a prominent part in our day to day evangelism, but we use the prophecies relating to the Messiah almost every day we go out to speak to people about the gospel. It is the simplest and yet most effective argument for the inspiration of scripture. We have yet to hear a valid, sensible answer to it from an unbeliever, and we would urge you to familiarise yourself with the following passages and have them at your fingertips – you will be glad you did.

There are prophecies relating to the birth of the Messiah, His life, miracles and teaching, but the ones that are particularly clear and compelling are those relating to His death. The two we make most use of are these:

(i) The Bible prophesied *how* He would die, Psalm 22;

(ii) The Bible prophesied *why* He would die, Isaiah 53.

We will briefly examine both of them and then give some practical pointers on how to employ them in conversation.

[113.] Adherents of other faiths often *take* certain passages in their scriptures as prophecies, but those passages weren't *given* as prophecies. They are usually statements lifted out of context and made to apply to current events. When I speak about prophecies I am speaking about passages that indisputably *predict* and *predate* events beyond human ability to anticipate or manipulate. The Bible is unique in this.

Examining the prophecies

(i) The Bible prophesied how He would die, Psalm 22.

Psalm 22 gives a vivid, accurate portrait of the crucifixion of the Lord Jesus Christ, and it does so from His point of view. It describes His spiritual suffering (vv. 1-3), His emotional suffering (vv. 4-11) and His physical suffering (vv. 12-21).

Tracing the outline of the figure in Psalm 22 we see:

- He is stripped of His garments (v. 18), and those garments are subsequently divided amongst onlookers.

- He is surrounded by Jewish oppressors (v. 12). The bull of Bashan is a straightforward picture – the bull was ceremonially clean in Israel; Bashan was the place where the finest of cattle were reared (e.g. Ezek. 39:18), and thus the bulls of Bashan would represent Jewish authority.

- He is surrounded by dogs (v. 16). The dogs symbolise the ceremonially-unclean Gentiles.

- These Gentiles pierce His hands and His feet (v. 16).

- His bones are out of joint (v. 14).

- He is exposed to burning heat, causing His strength to be dried up and His tongue to cling to His jaws (vv. 14-15).

- He is gazed at by wicked onlookers who have enclosed Him, as He suffers in weakness (vv. 16-17).

- He is laughed at (v. 7).

- He would suffer in daytime but it would also be in darkness (v. 2). Scripture records that there was darkness from 12:00 to 3:00 (Matt. 27:45; Mark 15:33; Luke 23:44). Thallus, a first-century historian, and Phlegon, a second-century historian, both referred to the darkness at the time of Christ's death, and tried to pass it off as an eclipse of the sun, which is impossible given when Christ died. Julius Africanus, the third-century church historian, had this to say:

> On the whole world there pressed a most fearful darkness; and the rocks were rent by an earthquake, and many places in Judea and other districts were thrown down. This darkness Thallus, in the third book of his History, calls, as appears to me without reason, an eclipse of the sun. For the Hebrews celebrate the passover on the 14th day according to the moon, and the passion of our Saviour falls on the day before the passover; but an eclipse of the sun takes place only when the moon comes under the sun. And it cannot happen at any other time but in the interval between the first day of the new moon and the last of the old, that is, at their junction: how then should an eclipse be supposed to happen when the moon is almost diametrically opposite the sun? Let opinion pass however; let it carry the majority with it; and let this portent of the world be deemed an eclipse of the sun, like others a portent only to the eye. Phlegon records that, in the time of Tiberius Caesar, at full moon, there was a full eclipse

of the sun from the sixth hour to the ninth – manifestly that one of which we speak. But what has an eclipse in common with an earthquake, the rending rocks, and the resurrection of the dead, and so great a perturbation throughout the universe? Surely no such event as this is recorded for a long period. But it was darkness induced by God, because the Lord happened then to suffer.[114]

- This sufferer experiences a deliverance that results in universal and eternal praise to God (vv. 27-31).

Nothing but crucifixion and no one but Christ fits the description of Psalm 22.

This is even more amazing given the fact that this was written about 500 years before crucifixion was invented.[115] As Brian Edwards wrote, "All this is too closely fulfilled in the crucifixion story to be casually overlooked."[116]

The accuracy of Psalm 22 can't be put down to human invention. It points to divine inspiration.

How difficult would it be to indicate the precise kind of death that a new, unknown religious leader would experience a thousand years from today? Could someone create and predict a new method of execution not currently known, one that

---

[114] *The Extant Writings of Julius Africanus*, 18.1, from the Master Christian Library.
[115] History shows that the Persians were the first to use this means of execution in the late sixth century BC, http://www.britannica.com/topic/crucifixion-capital-punishment. Herodotus records Darius impaling 3,000 leading men when he overcame the Babylonians in 519 BC (The History of Herodotus, vol. 1, iii, 159). Other ancient cultures would hang a dead body on a tree, but this is not crucifixion (e.g. Gen. 40:18-19; Deut. 21:22-23).
[116] Brian H. Edwards, *The Bible – an authentic book*, Day One Publications, 2015, p. 100.

wouldn't even be invented for hundreds of years? That's what King David did in 1000 BC when he wrote Psalm 22.[117]

We will move on to our next passage.

(ii) The Bible prophesied why He would die, Isaiah 53.

The prophecy of Isaiah was written in the 8th century BC.[118] Look at some of the details:

- This servant is despised and rejected by His people (53:3).

- He is condemned by an unjust trial (53:8).

- He is led submissively to execution (53:7).

- He is treated as a criminal and condemned with criminals (53:12).

- We find reference to piercing, bruising, punishment and stripes (53:5). The language of verse 5 is language associated with crucifixion. "Wounded" is "pierced through," and the stripe is that which is caused by a scourge.[119]

- He was terribly disfigured (52:14). The appearance of the servant in both His face and His form causes horror.

---

[117] John Ankerberg & John Weldon, *Fast Facts on Defending your Faith*, ATRI Publishing, 2013, loc 1011.
[118] See Gleason Archer, *New International Encyclopaedia of Bible Difficulties*, loc 6689.
[119] These are words associated with the physical suffering and crucifixion of the Lord, and yet the passage shows that they go beyond anything imposed upon Him by men. It is referring to suffering visited upon Him by God (53:10). But the point is that the language is associated with crucifixion.

- He was to be buried with criminals, but was associated with a rich man in His death (53:9).[120]

- His days have been prolonged (v.10). The servant dies, but then lives again. More on that in chapter 11.

As I spoke to a man about this, he interrupted me by shouting, "That's impossible. How could they have written about those things before they happened?" He was exactly right – it is humanly impossible to give such a detailed account hundreds of years in advance, but "the things which are impossible with men are possible with God" (Luke 18:27).

Employing the prophecies

Here is an example of a conversation we frequently have with people in which we use the evidence from fulfilled prophecy.

- **Hello. We are just giving out some literature about the relevance and reliability of the Bible's message. Have you any interest in that kind of thing?**

- No, not really, to be honest.

- **Oh, right. Do you ever think about what happens after death, if there is any afterlife or anything?**

- No, I don't think about that.

[120.] *Wicked* is a plural word and *rich* is singular.

- **Seriously? I would have thought everyone thinks about it at some point. Well, what do you think would happen to you if you died now?**

- No one knows. We just have to wait and see.

- **I would agree that if we were just left to ourselves then we couldn't be sure and we would just have to wait and see, but I don't think we have been left to ourselves. What we are telling people is that there are good reasons to believe that the Bible is the word of God.**

- You can't prove that.

- **Well, actually, I would like to give it a go, and it will only take two minutes. Will you let me?**

- Right, go ahead.

- **Okay, I'm going to read a passage here. [Read Psalm 22:14-18 and/or Isaiah 53:3-7. For this example we'll use Psalm 22.] Have you any idea what that was about?**

- The crucifixion of Jesus.

- **Yes, it's pretty clear, isn't it? Stripped of His garments, His hands and feet pierced, His bones out of joint, surrounded by a hostile crowd – it's obviously the crucifixion.**

- Right, so what's your point?

- **The point is that this passage was written hundreds of years before Jesus was born, and hundreds of years before crucifixion was even invented, yet we have no difficulty identifying what it's about.**

- How do you know it was written before He was born?

- **Good question. This passage is in the Hebrew Scriptures – the Old Testament. There's no way the Christians could have (or would have) inserted a whole section into all the scrolls of the Old Testament without anyone noticing. That's why there is no Jew who would say that this passage has been invented by Christians. Do you see what I mean?**

- Yeah, okay. I'm not sure what to make of it.

- **Suppose I told you that tomorrow, at 2:34pm that someone was going to call at your house, and I gave you a description of his clothes and appearance, and at 2:34pm tomorrow a man comes to your door matching in every way the description I had given, what would you think?**

- I would think you'd set it up!

- **Of course you would! There's no way something like that could just be a lucky guess. But look at what we've read – who set this up? And this is just one of many prophecies we could look at – there are loads of them. Who gave these writers the telescope to look down ages of time to events they could not** have naturally known or cleverly anticipated? How do you account for this?

- Hmmm. I don't know.

- **The only answer that makes any sense and fits the facts is the answer the Bible itself gives, "All Scripture is given by inspiration of God ..."**

- I see what you're saying, but it's not really my cup of tea.

- **I understand that, but the thing is, if there is good evidence that the Bible is God's word then you really can't afford to ignore it. This book, which has proven itself to be able to speak with accuracy and authority about the future speaks about your future and mine. It tells us that death is not the end, there is a God to meet, an eternity to face and a judgment to come, and because of our sin against God we are in danger of hell forever. We need to take that seriously.**

- Yeah, that's serious stuff.

- **It is, but listen, the Bible not only prophesied how Christ would die, it prophesied why He would die – to take the punishment we deserve so that we could go free, and if we agree with God about the problem of our sin and trust in Christ as the answer to the problem then the record of our guilt will be entirely and eternally cleared, and you will know in your own experience the reality of salvation. Do you think this is worth considering?**

- I'll give it some thought. Thanks.

Objections

The objections you will get to these prophecies are few and weak. All you need to be able to show is that the prophecies *predate* and *predict* Christ's crucifixion. As we have seen, the prophecies clearly predict Christ's crucifixion, and there is no doubt they predate it. Whatever objections Jews have to Jesus being the Messiah, the idea that Christians made up Psalm 22 and Isaiah 53 isn't among them. The Christians wouldn't and couldn't have tampered with the Hebrew Scriptures to insert these passages. And furthermore, the discovery of these passages among the Dead Sea Scrolls eliminates any last lingering doubt anyone could have on the matter.

In our evangelism we have seen Messianic prophecies evaporate the scepticism of the sceptic, and demolish the criticism of the critic. Presenting these prophecies has led people to be open to hear the gospel and has even resulted in salvation. It is a powerful tool, an effective weapon, a great resource, and simple to use.

2. The power of the Bible

"I see what you're saying, but there are just so many interpretations of the Bible." This is one of the standard responses we get from people when we present the gospel to them. It is a defensive manoeuvre intended to take the pressure off them a bit – "Look, you seem so sure that you're right, and I don't have any answers, but there are people who study the Bible more than you who come up with completely different opinions. Who's to say who is right?"

If discovering the truth of the Bible were just a matter of getting the right interpretation, then this objection would possibly have some force, but the Bible claims that a person can enter into new life through Christ now, and this is something you have experienced. You have known the life-changing power and the soul-satisfying reality of the gospel. This is not mere theory, you know it is real.

Your own testimony is a very powerful evangelistic tool, whether you are witnessing to atheists, cultists or people from other religions. You will find many opportunities to use your testimony in your outreach if you are ready. You might object that you don't have a very interesting story of conversion, but the point is not to speak about what you did or what the devil did. The point of a story of conversion is to speak about what Christ did. Whether you were saved in prison or primary school, the Lord has done something amazing in your life.

Take time to write out and memorise your own testimony and get it trimmed down so that you can deliver it in less than a minute. You should tell briefly why you wanted to be saved, how you were saved, and what it means to you now. Not only does your story show the reality of salvation in 3D and living colour, but it is an engaging and inoffensive way of communicating the gospel. You are not preaching *at* someone, saying, "*You* need this!" You are relating your experience, saying, "*I* needed this." And in telling why you needed salvation, you will be teaching them that they need it too. Let me show you how this typically works.

- **Hi there. We're giving out these booklets presenting the Christian gospel. Would you be interested in that kind of thing?**

- I can't think of anything I would be less interested in.

- **Okay, I understand that. It's not something I would have naturally been into either, but then an amazing thing happened.**

- Uh-huh?

- **Yes, I realised one day that I had broken God's law, and I needed God's forgiveness or I would bear the punishment for my sins forever. I knew that Jesus Christ had paid the penalty for sin on the cross, so I put my trust in Him to save me, and, just as the Bible promised, He has given me new life, so that I am now interested in things that once were as dry as dust to me. It is a real thing and a wonderful thing to be saved, and if it's real then it's something everyone needs.**

- Yeah, well, I'm just not interested in it.

- **Okay, but do you understand that if this is real then it's really serious?**

- Yes, if it's real.

- **And that's the thing, I'm telling you from my own experience, this is real. I've loads of evidence that it's real, and I'm more than happy to show it to you, but I'm not just weighing up evidence – this is something I have personally experienced; the Bible doesn't just promise heaven when you die, it promises new life right now, and if it delivers on that promise, that's good reason to believe it will deliver on all its promises.**

- Okay, but what about ...

Often when the door is shutting, a word of testimony can get it open again (literally and metaphorically). And even if the conversation goes no further than you telling of your salvation experience, it is worth it. You are leaving something with them that will stay with them, and we can trust God to use it.

In Mark 2:1-12, when the Lord Jesus pronounced that the paralysed man's sins were forgiven, the people around didn't believe a word of it. The Lord then exercised divine power in the man's life to prove that He did indeed have the authority to forgive sins. That miracle validated His word. Likewise, the message of the gospel doesn't just promise forgiveness for those who trust Christ as Saviour. If it did, then the spectre of doubt might always be lurking in the shadows: "Have you interpreted this correctly?" It says Christ will exercise divine power and grant divine life to the believer. The Christian is in the happy position of being able to see in his own life that Christ has delivered on His promise. The Christian has an interest in things that no one is naturally interested in, a desire for things that no one naturally desires. Christians are comfortable in activities that once made them most uncomfortable. The gospel makes a real difference in the lives of those who receive it. It gives new life now – you don't have to wait and see.

Any time people encountered the healing power of the word of the Lord, nothing could shake their confidence in it. The blind man who was healed (John 9) faced a lot of questions he couldn't answer, but he was living proof of this – there is power in the word of the Lord.

What about?

Even though you have given a positive case for the Bible being the word of God, there may be some push back. Don't panic. You don't have to be an expert on all the potential objections. You just need to remind yourself and the person that you are speaking with that you have presented positive evidence for your view. If you encounter an objection and you don't have the answer, try something like this (and keep the tone friendly and relaxed):

That's a question I've never thought of before. But just remember, I have given you proof that the Bible is God's word; all you've done is shown that I don't know everything (and I could have told you that anyway). You've asked a good question, and if it is something you really want to know the answer to then I'm more than happy to do some investigation and get back to you, but do you see that your question hasn't addressed the evidence I've offered?[121]

This isn't a dodge or a trick; it's a perfectly reasonable way to proceed. If the police have found overwhelming evidence for the guilt of a certain man, one or two unanswered questions can't overturn that evidence, and it would be a foolish jury that would acquit a man on the grounds that not every single loose end had been tied up.

We will briefly cover two objections that are quite common:

1. The morality of the Bible

It used to be that the Bible was known as the "Good Book," and those who believed the Bible were viewed by society as moral people. Society has changed. Any book that commands genocide, condemns homosexuality and condones slavery is a bad book, and any person who follows such a book is a bad person. This is how many people view the Bible and Bible-believers.

When we encounter someone with moral objections to the Bible we typically proceed in the following way:

[121.] Even if you have an answer to their question, don't feel that you need to chase every stick they throw. Especially if after answering a question they immediately produce another and another. You could say something like this: "That's a great question, and I've thought about it myself. I do have an answer but before I give it to you, I would like to know what you think about the evidence I've offered, is that okay?"

First – consider the facts

Point out that dislike of the Bible doesn't remove the evidence that it is the word of God. This is the primary issue, and pointing this out usually keeps the discussion on the facts. So you could say something like this:

I completely understand your point of view, and I'm happy to talk to you about that issue, but can you see that just because you don't like something that doesn't mean it's not true. I have offered you what I think is proof that the Bible is God's word, and so maybe we should deal with that first. Those issues you have raised are in a specific context which I think helps us understand them a lot better, but the first thing is to establish whether the Bible is God's word.

Second – challenge the foundation

If someone rejects the God of the Bible then they have no moral foundation to condemn any behaviour as wrong (more on this in chapter 9). They are merely imposing their own cultural tastes on others and condemning them for not living according to 21st century western values. The vast majority of people in the world and throughout history have not thought that the values so prized and vaunted in our society (personal autonomy, sexual freedom, individual happiness) really constitute the ultimate purpose and supreme good for humanity.

I urge people to consider that their problem with some texts might be based on an unexamined belief in the superiority of their historical moment over all others. We must not universalise our time any more than we should universalise our culture. Think of the implication of the very term 'regressive'. To reject the Bible as regressive is to assume that you have now arrived at the ultimate historic moment, from which all that is regressive and progressive can be discerned. That belief is surely as narrow and exclusive as the views in the Bible you regard as offensive.

Consider the views of contemporary British people and how they differ from the views of their ancestors, the Anglo-Saxons, a thousand years ago. Imagine that both are reading the Bible and they come to the Gospel of Mark, chapter 14. First they read that Jesus claims to be the Son of Man, who will come with angels at the end of time to judge the whole world according to his righteousness (verse 62). Later they read about Peter, the leading apostle, who denies his master three times and at the end even curses him to save his skin (verse 71). Yet later Peter is forgiven and restored to leadership (Mark 16:7; John 21:15ff.). The first story will make contemporary British people shudder. It sounds so judgemental and exclusive. However, they will love the story about how even Peter can be restored and forgiven. The first story will not bother the Anglo-Saxons at all. They know all about Domesday, and they are glad to get more information about it! However, they will be shocked at the second story. Disloyalty and betrayal at Peter's level must never be forgiven, in their view. He doesn't deserve to live, let alone become the foremost disciple. They will be so appalled by this that they will want to throw the Bible down and read no more of it. ...

How can we use our time's standard of 'progressive' as the plumbline by which we decide which parts of the Bible are valid and which are not? ... To stay away from Christianity because part of the Bible's teaching is offensive to you assumes that if there is a God he wouldn't have any views that upset you. Does that belief make sense?[122]

Third – clear the fog

If someone is genuinely troubled by the Bible commanding the slaughter of the Canaanites or the condemnation of homosexuality, or the "condoning" of slavery, keep the following issues in mind.

Slaughter of the Canaanites

As far as the Canaanites were concerned, depravity was rampant,[123] warning was given and the way was open for repentance and deliverance (see Rahab for a case in point). They were not singled out because of their ethnicity so this was not genocide, it was judgment. Also, archaeological excavations at Jericho and Ai show no evidence of civilian populations.

Given what we know about Canaanite life in the Bronze Age, Jericho and Ai were military strongholds. In fact, Jericho guarded the travel routes from the Jordan Valley up to

---

[122.] Timothy Keller, *The Reason for God: Belief in an Age of Scepticism*, Hodder & Stoughton, 2008, pp. 111-112.

[123.] See Paul Copan, *Is God a Moral Monster?: Making Sense of the Old Testament God*, Baker Books, 2011, pp. 159-161.

population centers in the hill country. It was the first line of defense at the junction of three roads leading to Jerusalem, Bethel, and Orpah. That means that Israel's wars here were directed toward government and military instalments; this is where the king, the army, and the priesthood resided.[124]

Most of the women in such places would have been in the same line of business as Rahab. There would not have been many families in these places, and thus the language calling for the destruction of men, women and children, young and old "was merely stock ancient Near Eastern language that could be used even if women and young and old weren't living there."[125]

Another issue to bear in mind is that the language of destruction is often used in a context in which expulsion from the land is clearly meant (e.g. Deut. 9:3-5). Indeed, God said He would do to Israel what He did to the nations if they broke His covenant (Deut. 8:20), and when Israel's judgment came, it was expulsion from the land (Deut. 4:26-28). This exile was described and pictured as death (e.g. Ezek. 37:1-14; Jer. 31:15-17).

Condemnation of homosexuality

It is rare to speak to a young person today without the subject of homosexuality arising. They simply cannot understand why anyone would be against two people who

[124] Ibid., pp. 175-176.
[125] Ibid., p. 176.

love each other being together. There are a couple of things to keep in mind here.

(a) Marriage is safe

God's laws are for the flourishing of humanity. Creatorial marriage, i.e. the monogamous, exclusive, life-long committed union of a man and a woman, is for the emotional and physical wellbeing of both involved. It is also for the good of any children that may result from that union and for the good of society. Any deviation from God's plan carries with it huge emotional and physical risks.[126] When you talk to young people about this subject you should do your best to communicate that it is out of compassion to humanity that God places boundaries. He has created humans to function and flourish a certain way. When we don't function as He intended, we don't flourish as He intended.

(b) Marriage is significant

Marriage communicates a message – the union of a man and a woman in marriage symbolises the union of Christ and His church (Eph. 5:25-27), and thus any tampering of that distorts something very precious to God. In addition, under the theocracy of Israel, there were severe penalties for sexual impurity to reflect the holiness of God and

---

[126.] See, for example, Frank Turek, *Correct, not Politically Correct: How Same-Sex Marriage Hurts Everyone.*

to preserve the integrity of the genealogies to ensure the Messiah's right to the throne was evident.

Slavery

The thing to point out here is that the slavery spoken about in scripture is not the kind of slavery that existed in the southern United States. The slavery in Israel was indentured service. If you were strapped for cash or in over your head in debt, you could put yourself into the employ of your creditor and work for him, getting your lodgings and food in his home. At the end of your period of servitude you could go free, with sufficient resources to stand on your own two feet.[127]

When it comes to slavery in the Roman empire:

> [T]here was not a great difference between slaves and the average free person. Slaves were not distinguishable from others by race, speech or clothing. They looked and lived like most everyone else, and were not segregated from the rest of society in any way. From a financial standpoint, slaves made the same wages as free labourers, and therefore were not usually poor. Also, slaves could accrue enough personal capital to buy themselves out. Most important of all, very few slaves were slaves for life. Most could reasonably hope to be manumitted within ten or fifteen years, or by their late thirties at the latest.[128]

[127.] See Copan, *Is God a Moral Monster?*, chapters 12-13.
[128.] Keller, *The Reason for God*, p. 110.

The Bible explicitly condemns the stealing of human beings (1 Tim. 1:10), which is a condemnation of the whole enterprise of New World slavery and the African slave trade. That is why it was biblically-faithful, committed Christians who led the fight against it.

2. The make-up of the Bible

Rejected texts

What about all the "gospels" that the church rejected? Since the success of Dan Brown's *The Da Vinci Code*, the idea of the early church being in a political power struggle, perpetually embroiled in controversy, has become popular. The facts tell a different story. When someone asks why the church rejected certain "gospels" I point out that every single Gospel that goes back to the first century is in the Bible. There is not one of these so-called gospels that have been discovered that goes back to the first century. Why then would you ever want to take the word of someone who wasn't there, shows no knowledge of the land, no familiarity with the customs, and communicates a worldview that is completely foreign to first century Judaism?[129] This has always been sufficient to neutralise any objections on the selection of the Gospels.

[129.] For more on the Gnostic Gospels see the relevant chapter in Lee Strobel, *The Case for the Real Jesus, A Journalist Investigates Current Attacks on the Identity of Christ*, Zondervan.

Distorted texts

Has the Bible not been corrupted? How do we know that what we have today is what was originally written? When it comes to the Old Testament, its integrity is guaranteed by the *quality* of the copies. Professional scribes meticulously copied the scriptures, and the quality of their work has been confirmed by the discovery of the Dead Sea Scrolls. The integrity of the New Testament is guaranteed by the *quantity* of the manuscripts. The early Christians sought to copy the documents as quickly as possible and spread them as widely as possible. This means there was no person or group that has custody of the text – no one had the ability or authority to gather all the texts and tamper with them. The transmission of the New Testament was not like the game of Chinese Whispers, in which the original message is passed down one line, and if mistakes or changes are made there's no way of correcting them. The multiple streams of transmission ensure that changes or mistakes can be identified even without having the original because everyone wouldn't make the same changes or mistakes at the same place. But Tertullian, writing in approximately AD 180, seemed to indicate that the original letters of the apostles were still accessible for checking:

> *Come now, you who would indulge a better curiosity, if you would apply it to the business of your salvation, run over [to] the apostolic churches, in which the very thrones of the apostles are still pre-eminent in their places, in which their*

own authentic writings are read, uttering the voice and representing the face of each of them severally.[130]

In any event, there is absolutely no reason to be sceptical about the trustworthiness of the text of scripture, and every reason to be confident.

Conclusion

We haven't gone into detail on the answers to these objections for the simple reason we rarely need to. No amount of corruption of the text is going to result in the fulfilment of prophecy or the transformation of lives, and if the person you are talking to is fair-minded, he will acknowledge that. If he's not fair-minded then he's not really looking for answers anyway.

Imagine someone looking at a bumblebee buzzing around. She thinks to herself, "I can't figure out how that thing can fly. It doesn't seem to make sense." Since, however, the bumblebee flies, she knows there will be an answer. She's not going to say, "I still can't figure out how the bumblebee flies so I don't believe that it does."

The two arguments we have looked at (the prophecies of scripture and the power of scripture) provide not merely good evidence, and not even overwhelming evidence, but actual proof of the inspiration of scripture – you can see it right in front of you and experience it for yourself. This

---

[130.] Tertullian, *De Praescriptione Haereticorum*, chapter 36, Schaff's translation. See https://bible.org/article/did-original-new-testament-manuscripts-still-exist-second-century-0 for Daniel Wallace's discussion on this.

means that any questions we can't answer must have an answer. The bumblebee has proven its flying ability; the Bible has proven its divine authority.

So be ready with your positive case, and when objections arise don't get defensive or deceptive. Be sympathetic, but point out that they don't dent your case. You can agree to discuss those objections later, set a date to meet up, or direct them to the resources we've referenced, then steer the conversation back to what you do know rather than what you don't know. You know that the Bible is God's word, and you can show that it is too, so proclaim it with confidence and authority. "It shall not return ... void" (Isa. 55:11).

Chapter 8

SCIENCE

I don't believe in God, I just go by science.

There are some ideas that are so embedded in the subconscious of a culture that they are assumed and aired without a challenge ever being anticipated. One of those notions is that science has disproved God. It's as firmly established as the "fact" that Vikings wore helmets with horns, that bats are blind, and that bulls hate the colour red.[131]

If you get involved in personal evangelism, you will meet someone who says, "I prefer to base my beliefs on science," or something similar. Where do we go from here?

What to ask

Lots of Christians have the idea that it is their responsibility to refute every claim an unbeliever makes. Just remember, whoever makes the claim bears the burden. If someone says science disproves God then it's up to him to prove

---

[131.] They didn't, they aren't, and they don't.

that; it's not up to you to disprove it. So use the question we talked about in the previous section of this book; ask, "What do you mean by that? In what particular ways do you think science disproves God or the gospel?" And if he offers something about evolution you could ask, "How do you know that's true?" This is usually enough to expose the fact that the person you are talking to is merely parroting a popular meme rather than expressing anything substantive.

You could also ask, "If science disproves God, then how come some of the greatest scientists throughout history and across the world are Christians? If these people see no conflict between science and God, what do you know that they don't?"[132] Unless they are extremely arrogant, they will have to acknowledge that science therefore mustn't disprove God's existence. If you want to move the subject elsewhere, you can then say, "Given that many Christians and atheists are leading scientists, let's leave science and talk about ..."

However, when I encounter this response I sometimes prefer to use it as an opportunity to go on the offensive. Let me outline the approach and then we'll go back and fill it in with a sample conversation.

What to attack

The notion that science can disprove God is not even possible in principle. Science is the study of the physical universe; it cannot therefore tell you that a nonphysical

---

[132.] e.g. https://en.wikipedia.org/wiki/List_of_Christians_in_science_and_technology.

being doesn't exist. That would be like someone examining every square inch of a building and telling you, "There is no designer or builder because I've searched the whole building and they aren't here." This assumes the designer and builder are part of the building. A sensible person would not expect to see the designer or builder in the building, but he would expect to see evidence of their work. So it is with the universe – God is not part of His creation. Unlike all the gods of mythology, the God of scripture is not derived from matter.

Furthermore, just because we can understand how the universe works doesn't mean God has been disproved. Indeed, the fact that the universe is intelligible is a clear pointer towards God.

The illustration John Lennox makes use of is apt here.

Take a Ford motor car. It is conceivable that someone from a remote part of the world, who was seeing one for the first time and who knew nothing about modern engineering, might imagine that there is a god (Mr Ford) inside the engine, making it go. He might further imagine that when the engine ran sweetly it was because Mr Ford inside the engine liked him, and when it refused to go it was because Mr Ford did not like him. Of course, if he were subsequently to study engineering and take the engine to pieces, he would discover that there is no Mr Ford inside it. Neither would it take much intelligence for him to see that he did not need to introduce Mr Ford as an explanation for its working. His grasp of the impersonal principles of internal combustion would be altogether enough to explain how the engine works. So far, so good. But if he then decided that his understanding of the principles of how the engine works made it impossible to believe in the existence of Mr Ford who designed the engine in the first place, this would be patently false – in philosophical terminology he would be committing a category mistake. Had there never been a Mr Ford to design the mechanisms, none would exist for him to understand.

It is likewise a category mistake to suppose that our understanding of the impersonal principles according to which the universe works makes it either unnecessary or impossible to believe in the existence of a personal creator who designed, made, and upholds the universe. In other words, we should not confuse the mechanisms by which the universe works either with its cause or its upholder.[133]

So the notion that science has disproved God is popular but misguided. The reality is, the more the universe is studied, the more evident His existence is.

What to advance

There is a positive case to make. Keep the following two points in mind:

1. Science points towards a God
2. Science points towards the God of scripture

[133.] John C. Lennox, *God's Undertaker: Has Science Buried God?*, Lion, 2007, pp. 44.

1. Science points towards a God

As David looked up at the beauty of creation, he couldn't help singing, "The heavens declare the glory of God" (Ps. 19:1). This has only become more true and obvious as science has advanced and knowledge has increased.

There are three facts of science that are worth having at the ready, and they will serve you well no matter how knowledgeable the person you are talking to happens to be.

We live in a fathomable universe

What way would the universe have to be for science to be even possible? Two features are required:

i   A rational creation

ii Rational creatures

i. A rational creation

If the universe tumbled into existence without a creator/ designer then why would anyone suppose that it would operate according to laws that would be consistent and discoverable? To quote from Lennox again:

> *One person who drew attention to this circumstance ... was the eminent historian of science and mathematician Sir Alfred North Whitehead. Observing that medieval Europe in 1500 knew less than Archimedes in the third century BC and yet by 1700 Newton had written his masterpiece,* Principia Mathematica, *Whitehead asked the obvious question:*

How could such an explosion of knowledge have happened in such a relatively short time? His answer: "modern science must come from the medieval insistence on the rationality of God ... My explanation is that the faith in the possibility of science, generated antecedently to the development of modern scientific theory, is an unconscious derivative from medieval theology". C. S. Lewis' succinct formulation of Whitehead's view is worth recording: "Men became scientific because they expected law in nature and they expected law in nature because they believed in a lawgiver"[134]

ii. Rational creatures

For science to be possible, there needs to be a creature that is capable of rational thought, but if atheism is true then everything in the universe is physical and reacts according to the laws of physics and chemistry. This would mean that there is no such thing as rationality. Every thought of the mind would only be the deterministic by-product of chemical processes over which we have no control. As Frank Turek says, it's not merely "that science supports theism but theism supports science. In other words, theism makes doing science possible. We wouldn't be able to do science reliably if atheism were true."[135]

We live in a finite universe

Up until the previous century atheists always believed

[134.] Lennox, *God's Undertaker*, p. 20.
[135.] Frank Turek, *Stealing from God, Why atheists need God to make their case*, NavPress, 2014, p. 145.

that the universe had eternally existed. That view was wrenched from their grasp by several independent scientific discoveries that proved that the universe had a beginning a finite time ago.[136]

Science is really the search for causes to explain effects. When I ask people about the origin of the universe they will often say that the cause is the Big Bang, but this is confused. The Big Bang is not the cause, it is the *effect* that needs a cause. The Big Bang didn't bring the universe into existence; it is just the name for the event of the universe coming into existence. A conversation I had with a young man illustrates this point. I had knocked his door to invite him to gospel meetings and here is how the conversation went:

- **Hello, we're just letting people know about some meetings that are taking place to explain how we can be sure of heaven when life is over. Have you any interest in that kind of thing?**

- No, I haven't. I'm an atheist.

- **Why's that?**

- Because of science.

- **Oh, right. So how do you explain how the universe came into existence?**

- The Big Bang.

[136.] For five independent lines of evidence for the beginning of the universe see Norman L. Geisler and Frank Turek, *I Don't Have Enough Faith to Be an Atheist*, Crossway, 2004, pp. 73-94.

- **Okay. Tell me this, why did you come to the door?**

- What?

- **Why did you come to the door?**

- Because you knocked it.

- **Right, so you heard a bang, and you didn't just say, "Oh, there's a bang." You immediately concluded that something or someone caused it. You see, the bang didn't cause anything, the bang was caused. Why is it when there's a little bang you conclude someone is there, but when there's a Big Bang you say no one is there?**

- I'll have to go back and check my physics books!

- **But your physics books aren't going to help you. They will tell you that at the Big Bang all of matter came into existence. Whatever caused that to happen can't be anything material. Physics is no good if there is nothing physical. The cause of the universe coming into existence must be non-physical.**

- Come on in.

This sceptical atheist invited me into his house to speak to him and his girlfriend about God. I got a wonderful opportunity to present the gospel to them. What opened the door was a very simple, yet powerful, argument. Here it is laid out:

Whatever begins to exist has a cause;
The universe began to exist;
Therefore, the universe has a cause.[137]

If the first two lines are true then the conclusion must be true. If you meet someone who denies either of the first two lines then you can accuse them of being anti-science (and see how they like it).

Our first premise is obviously true. If it is denied then science is doomed. The scientist would be laughed out of the lab if he said he had come to the conclusion that what he had been studying under the microscope had just appeared out of nothing without a cause. It is no less ridiculous to say that something the size of the universe just appeared out of nothing without a cause.

The second premise of the syllogism is certainly true. Logically and empirically, there can be no doubt that the universe came into existence. Even if people appeal to the increasingly popular multiverse as an explanation for our universe, the multiverse must have had a beginning.[138] Anyone who denies the second premise is swimming against mainstream science, and if your objector has raised science as an argument against God, then he's hardly likely to want to swim in that direction.

---

[137] This is called the *Kalam Cosmological Argument*, and has been developed by William Lane Craig. For more on it see chapter 4 of William Lane Craig, *On Guard: Defending your Faith with Reason and Precision*, David C. Cook, 2010, or his *Reasonable Faith: Christian Truth and Apologetics*, Third Edition, Crossway, 2008, loc 1850-2647.

[138] See Craig, *On Guard*, pp. 93-94.

Given the truth of lines one and two, the conclusion follows inescapably. The universe had a cause.

What cause could be adequate to bring about the effect of the entire universe coming into existence? As I said in my discussion with the sceptic, the cause can't be something material, because science has shown that matter is not eternal. It must therefore be non-physical, but what kind of a non-physical entity could bring about the creation of the whole universe? It must be a personal,[139] powerful, timeless and spaceless entity. In a word, God.

I remember hearing a presentation by an atheist who was asked what it would take for him to believe in God. He replied by saying that if something appeared out of nothing in front of him at that moment, he would believe in God. Notice how his test for God depends on the rock-solid truth of the first line of our argument. If something popped into existence in front of him, he wouldn't shrug his shoulders and say, "These things happen." The odd thing is that this atheist had just been speaking about the second line of the argument – he affirmed that the universe came into existence out of nothing. The question is, why would *something* coming into existence out of nothing *now* prove God, but *everything* coming into existence out of nothing *a long time ago* doesn't?

[139.] The reason why the cause must be personal is because if the cause was impersonal then it couldn't choose to act, meaning that the effect would have existed as long as the cause existed. The only way you could have an eternal cause and a temporal effect is if the cause chose to create.

We live in a fine-tuned universe

The fact that we live in a finite universe points to a powerful creator, but the fact that we live in a fine-tuned universe points to an intelligent designer. We don't use this argument very often in conversation, but we will mention it briefly, because the late Christopher Hitchens said that he and his New Atheist colleagues (Dawkins, Harris and Dennett) agreed that it is the best argument "from the other side".[140] It merits a mention and is handy to be aware of.[141]

There are lots of discoveries coming from the realms of physics and biology that defy a naturalistic explanation and cry out for a transcendent cause. If, like me, you aren't an expert in physics or biology, it's important that you don't pretend you are. But we don't need to wade into the details.

Physics

Physicists have found that the existence of the universe is balanced on a very thin tightrope in that there are dozens of physical constants and quantities such that, had they been the slightest bit different, there would have been no stars, no planets and no chemistry.[142]

Imagine a factory with lots of machines. There is a control panel with dozens of dials. Each dial has trillions of possible settings, and for the machinery to work, each

---

[140.] https://www.youtube.com/watch?v=GDJ9BL38PrI&t=3s.

[141.] See Craig, On Guard, ch. 5 for more detail.

[142.] The fine-tuned constants include the force of gravity, the electromagnetic force, and the strong and weak nuclear forces. The fine-tuned quantities include the entropy level of the universe and the ratio of protons to electrons. See http://www.reasons.org/articles/fine-tuning-for-life-in-the-universe-aug-2006 for more.

dial has to be exactly set to the right value. If one of the dials is the slightest bit off then the machines can't work. If you arrived at the factory and found all the machines working, would you conclude that someone had come in and randomly spun all the dials and landed on the right value for each one? Of course not. But this is what atheists are forced to conclude about the universe. (In fact, it is worse – they have to conclude that the factory came from nothing, the machinery was undesigned, and when this control panel popped into existence it just so happened to have the right values.)

To avoid the inference to design, many atheists opt for the multiverse. The multiverse is a universe generator that is pumping out universes all the time, and these universes all have different quantities and constants, so if this universe generator is continually cranking out universes then eventually it is going to hit on one that has all the right values. As we have said above, the multiverse can't get rid of the necessity of a creator, but can it do away with the necessity of a designer? Not at all. Something that can produce universes does sound like the kind of thing that would need a designer, but that's not all. The chances of producing a life-permitting universe remain overwhelmingly unlikely no matter how many efforts you have.

Imagine our factory again. Pretend there are just ten dials and a billion possible settings on each, and each dial must be set to a particular value to allow the machinery to work – if one dial is out by one setting then nothing works. You start at dial one and spin, if you get the right value you go on to dial two, and so on. Any time you hit the wrong value you have to back to dial one and start all over again. Do you think, no matter how often you try, you would ever get all ten dials to land on the right settings just by chance? The probability of this is one in 10^{90}. It isn't going to happen no matter how often you try. The odds don't improve on each effort; each time you try it you are just as unlikely to achieve it as the time before. To get that specified outcome you need to fix it. And our thought experiment is far more likely than the chance of randomly hitting all the right values for the existence of a life-permitting universe, because not only do we have more than ten dials, we have far more than a billion settings.[143]

Biology

Back in Darwin's day, it was supposed that a single cell was a simple thing, but research has shown it to be far from simple. The cell, which is the basis of life, containing about 100 million proteins of 20,000 different types, is really like a miniature motor car factory with loads of mini assembly lines and all the different parts performing different functions in a very busy but highly efficient way. A typical cell contains billions of units of DNA making up the chromosomes that make the machines that cause the cell to work. The

---

[143.] Physicists have estimated at least 30 different parameters (or dials) that have to be set just right, and the degree of accuracy to which they have to be set is mind-boggling. For example, the dial controlling the atomic weak force has 10^{100} settings, while the dial for the initial entropy of the universe has $10^{10(123)}$ settings (that's a 1 with 1,000,000,000,000,000,000,000,000,000,000,000,000,000,00 0,000,000,000,000,000,000,000,000,000,000,000,000,000,000,000,0 00,000,000,000,000,000 zeros after it)!

DNA can only be described in terms of language or code, and has been likened to a computer program; indeed, Bill Gates said DNA is far, far more advanced than any software Microsoft had created.[144] Every single one of the trillions of cells in the human body contains a database larger than the Encyclopaedia Britannica. But where does information come from? Who is the programmer? Who wrote the language and gave the code? Let's go back to our factory illustration and adjust it to make it relevant to biology. If you came along and discovered that all the computerised machinery was working, would you suppose that all the pieces of the machinery came together without any design or forethought, and there was no intelligence involved in programming the computers? If there is information, it has come from intelligence. Programming requires a programmer.

The more we investigate the realms of physics and biology, the more we see the fingerprints of God on His creation. In light of such evidence, no one can accuse the believer of blind faith.

2. Science points towards the God of scripture

It's not just that science points towards some generic deity, science points specifically to the God of the Bible. How so?

There are many statements in the Bible about the universe that were not scientifically known at the time, but

---

[144.] Bill Gates, *The Road Ahead*, cited in Lee Strobel, *The Case for a Creator: A Journalist Investigates Scientific Evidence That Points toward God*, Zondervan, 2004, p. 238.

scientists have come to make these grand discoveries that confirm what the Bible said.

Consider the following examples:[145]

- The universe began to exist. As we have said, this was not the prevailing view, whether of atheists or people from other faiths, but it's there in the very first statement of the Biblical story. Scientists were forced to acknowledge it nearly 3,500 years after Moses wrote it.

- Time began. This was established scientifically at the beginning of the twentieth century, but the Bible says that God created the ages (Heb. 1:2),[146] and that He existed "before all time" (Jude v. 25, ESV).

- The expansion of the universe – repeatedly the Bible hints at this 20th century discovery by speaking about God as the God who stretches out the heavens (see, e.g., Job 9:8; Ps. 104:2; Isa. 40:22).

- There are innumerable stars (Jer. 33:22). With only 3,000-5,000 stars being visible to the naked eye, it must have seemed strange that the Bible would put the number of stars in the same category as the number of grains of sand. With the advanced technology available today we now know there are more stars than grains of sand. The only strange thing about it now is how these ancient writers

---

[145]. For more examples and more detail see McCauley, *Prove It*, ch. 4.
[146]. Most translations say He made the "worlds", but the word literally means "ages".

knew there were so many stars if the Bible wasn't given by God.

- The earth hangs on nothing (Job 26:7). Contrary to all the strange ideas different cultures had, the oldest book in the Bible got it right.

- The water cycle (Eccl. 1:7). The water cycle was "discovered" in 1580 by Bernard Palissy, but Solomon said it first.

- There are paths in the sea (Ps. 8:8). It was Psalm 8 verse 8 that led Matthew Fontaine Maury (1806-1873) to seek and discover these paths.

Just this sprinkling of examples is usually enough to indicate to the person you are talking to that they shouldn't assume the Bible and science are at odds. As the agnostic astronomer, Robert Jastrow said:

> For the scientist who has lived by his faith in the power of reason, the story ends like a bad dream. He has scaled the mountain of ignorance; he is about to conquer the highest peak; as he pulls himself over the final rock, he is greeted by a band of theologians who have been sitting there for centuries.[147]

Science points to God, the God of scripture.

[147.] Robert Jastrow, *God and the Astronomers*, cited in Geisler & Turek, *I don't have enough Faith to be an Atheist*, p. 94.

What to avoid

There are some subjects I just don't get into when I am engaging with an unbeliever.

Dating of the universe

You may have very strong convictions regarding the age of the universe, and you might be able to defend those against all comers. That's fine. I don't consider it a profitable area of discussion in evangelism. There are God-fearing, inerrancy-affirming believers with differing views on when creation occurred based on what the Bible actually says, so I don't get into discussions with unbelievers on a subject that is an in-house debate. Whether the universe is old or young, the fact is it is not eternal, and that is the problem for the atheist.

Details of the universe

As I've said, I'm not an expert in science, so I can't get into an in-depth discussion on the intricacies of cutting-edge scientific theories. But even if you are an expert, I would still advise you not to go into detail. Why? Because I wouldn't want people to get the impression that you need a PhD in nuclear physics to see that God exists. I remember watching a discussion between an atheist and a Christian molecular biologist. The Christian gave a very detailed explanation about how there is no way the reproductive system of a whale could have come about by Darwinian evolution. It was fascinating, but the atheist was a bit overwhelmed with the barrage of information, and his response was along the lines of, "We are talking about the most important issue in life, and your evidence is a whale's reproductive system? Do I really need to be an expert in that to have evidence of God's existence?" I think it was a fair point. There is a lot riding on the question of God's existence; the evidence should be accessible to all.

If you aren't an expert on science, then make that clear if that is where the discussion is going, and don't let the person you're speaking with blind you with science. If you are out of your depth, just admit it and say something like:

That's all really interesting; at least I'm sure it would be if I could understand it. But the point I'm making is quite simple, not at all controversial, and it's conceded by the experts you would respect: the universe began to exist, and that includes quantum vacuums or whatever that was you said there. So my question is, is it more reasonable to believe that nothing caused the universe or something caused the universe?

Or you could try saying:

I really wouldn't be able to go into a detailed discussion, it's not something I've studied, but I'm interested in what is required for scientific investigation in the first place. If atheism is true then everything in the universe acts according to the laws of physics and chemistry, and that includes you and me; we are just collections of chemicals, and we have no more control over our actions than any other collection of chemicals. Chemicals don't choose their behaviour; they just do what they are determined to do. That seems to destroy the very foundation for the rationality needed to do science. Can you account for consciousness and rationality based on the view that you are nothing but matter acting according to physical law?

Or another approach I have taken is:

Clearly you know a lot about science, but it does seem to me that when we look at basic facts rather than involved speculations, the facts point one way. The universe is not eternal, there are loads of physical constants set just right to allow the universe to exist, the cell is not simple, it's complex, and life is built on information – DNA. None of that is controversial, and all of that is, at the very least, compatible with belief in God, but what about if I show you some evidence outside of science. What do you think of Jesus Christ?

Or finally:

I'm not an expert in science, but one thing that does interest me is that in the Bible there are many things stated that science didn't discover until centuries afterwards. It certainly gives credibility to the claim the Bible makes about itself that it came from God. Have you ever considered the evidence for the Bible?

Conclusion

Don't bluff, and don't let yourself be pulled into the minutiae of a particular field of science. There's no need. If someone has raised science as an objection to belief in God, then stick to these points we have looked at. This will allow you to not only diffuse the objection, but to use the objection to confront the person with the reality of their Creator.

Chapter 9

SUFFERING

I used to believe in God, but then we lost our baby.

This is the main objection to belief in God. It's something that everyone has wondered about, and something you certainly will face in presenting the gospel to others – "If God is so good, then why is the world so bad?"

Why does God permit wars, allow earthquakes, tolerate disease, watch babies die? It's a big question, but it's not one the Bible avoids. When something is wrong with your health, car, computer, or anything, you try to identify the cause and the cure. We all recognise that something is wrong with the world. The Bible explains why things went wrong (the cause) and what God is going to do about it (the cure). You don't get that anywhere else. Atheism obviously can't say that there is anything "wrong" with the world, because that demands a purpose and a standard (more on that later). The eastern all-is-one, reality-is-an-illusion faiths can't say that there is anything wrong with the world because, as Greg Koukl says, 'There cannot be a problem of evil, even in principle. As odd as it may seem, there is nothing wrong with the way things are. Everything just is. All-that-is is perfect at every moment. Or as one famous proponent of this view [Deepak Chopra] put it, "All is as it should be."'[148] Islam denies that Adam's sin affected the world or the human race in any way,[149] so redemption and restoration don't seem to fit the Muslim story. All non-Biblical worldviews either ignore or deny the problem. The Bible confronts it. The way the world *is* is not the way it *was*, nor is it the way it *will be*.

The *first* book in the Bible, Genesis, addresses directly how, when and where things went wrong. What is perhaps the *oldest* book in the Bible, Job, is an account of a man wrestling with the subject of why God allows suffering. The *biggest* book in the Bible, the book of Psalms, is full of complaints, questions, and appeals to God about the problem of pain and the prosperity of the wicked, and it is also brimming with the joyful hope that the Lord will turn things around and establish His glorious kingdom on earth. The *last* book in the Bible, Revelation, paints a beautiful picture of an eternity free from sin and a world free from suffering. So the Bible doesn't gloss over the problem. In fact, you could summarise the story of the Bible in a sentence by saying, *The Bible is about God redeeming fallen humanity*

[148.] Gregory Koukl, *The Story of Reality: How the World Began, How it Ends, and Everything Important that Happens in Between*, Zondervan, 2017, p. 62.
[149.] The Koran seems to teach that Adam and Eve were sent to earth as a result of their disobedience (Surah 2:36; 7:24; 20:123), and that death is not a result of sin (Surah 23:14-15).

and restoring fallen creation for His glory. In this statement the two sources of suffering are addressed: moral evil – fallen humanity will be redeemed; natural evil – fallen creation will be restored.

We will look at these two problems separately:

Moral Evil

Moral evil is the evil that is committed by humans. There are three things to keep in mind when you face this challenge.

Look upward

When someone challenges you with, "How could a good God allow the abduction and abuse of a little child?" don't begin by talking about free will and mysterious plans. All of that might be relevant and useful later, but that is not where to start. You need to show that the problem raised by the unbeliever doesn't undermine your worldview but his.[150]

The person who raises the challenges recognises a problem, but what kind of worldview allows for this kind of problem? It certainly isn't an atheistic worldview.

Evil is a departure from the way things ought to be, but if there is no God then there is no way things *ought* to be, there only is the way things *are*. If atheism were true, then the universe didn't tumble into existence with a set of rules,

---

[150.] Needless to say, if you are talking to someone whose child has been abducted you will not engage them in debate. This is assuming the person is merely asking the question, not a victim of the evil in question. In all your dealings with unbelievers it is vital you don't view them as opponents, but that you seek to connect with them.

and even if it did, what would make such rules binding on any of the living organisms that arose through the mindless process of Darwinian evolution?

The following sample conversation will illustrate the point.

- **Hello. We are giving out some literature about the biblical message of salvation. Do you ever think about that?**

- No, I've no interest in it.

- **Oh, right, do you believe in God?**

- Absolutely not.

- **Okay. Do you mind me asking, what reasons do you have for not believing in God?**

- Well, how could there be a God with all the evil in the world?

- **I see where you're coming from, but do you know what I think? The evil in the world doesn't disprove God's existence, it proves it.**

- How do you make that out?

- **What is evil?**

- Well, you know, murder, rape, child abuse ...

- **Yes, I agree those things are evil, but I'm not asking for examples, I'm asking for a definition.**

- It's bad stuff, doing things that are wrong.

- Okay, who says whether it's bad or wrong?

- Society – that's how we make laws.

- So is something only evil because society says it is? How then can there be an evil society or unjust laws? If someone takes a child to a desert island where there are no laws, courts or prisons, is it not just as evil for him to abuse that child there as here?

- Of course.

- So something isn't evil because we make a law against it, we make laws against things because they are evil. So if something isn't wrong because we say so, then why is it wrong?

- Well, it just is, we know it is. You don't need the Bible to know it's wrong to abuse a child.

- Absolutely, but if God doesn't exist, then there's no way things ought to be; there are no rules other than the ones we make up. But as you have said, we know there's a way we ought to behave; we know that there are things that are wrong whether there's a law against them or not. Richard Dawkins was being consistent with his atheism when he said there is "no evil and no good, nothing but blind, pitiless indifference." But we know that's not true. Evil is real; there is a way we ought to behave, and that can only be because there is a righteous God who has made us in His image and written the demands of His law on our heart.

Another point to keep in mind is that atheism can't even account for the freedom that is necessary for evil to exist. If a tree produces rotten fruit, we don't say that the tree is morally evil; when a rose produces thorns, we don't condemn it as wicked. Trees and flowers have no control over their actions, and they produce whatever their genes and environment combine to produce. Similarly, if atheism is true, then we are every bit as much physically determined as a tree or a flower. If there is no soul distinct from the body, no mind distinct from the brain, then there is no way we can control what we do. Every action is the result of a previous reaction – there is no such thing as free will.

If you begin by defending God's right to allow evil, you are granting the atheist the right to complain about something that his worldview gives him no right to complain about. Furthermore, in the face of such rampant evil in the world, he will likely find any attempts to justify God weak and insulting. What you should aim to do is take the ground out from under him and show that atheism gives him no hook to hang evil from, and every time he encounters evil he is encountering proof of a righteous God.

Now, things can get a bit confused in conversations on this subject. Here is a list of a few responses for you to watch out for.

Evolution explains morality

This is something that is often trotted out. The story goes like this – we have evolved to be a social species, and if we are to survive we have to get along with each other. Natural selection has therefore favoured creatures that display altruism and reciprocity, and that is why we feel those things are good and whatever militates against such things is bad.

This theory is full of problems. I won't go into all of them, but the foundational issue is this: evolution, even if it were true, at best could explain *why* we behave a certain way, but it couldn't say whether we *should* behave a certain way. As Frank Turek says, "How could a mutating genetic code have the moral authority to tell you how you *ought to* behave?"[151] According to the theory, all my desires and inclinations (selfishness as well as selflessness, cowardice as well as courage) are the result of natural selection acting on random mutations; you can't then say that evolution says one set of inclinations is good and another evil.

The Darwinian story doesn't explain morality, it explains it away. It doesn't tell us that selfishness and cowardice is wrong, it attempts to tell us why we *think* it's wrong. So the evolutionist is letting the cat out of the bag and telling the world that there is no objective morality; evolution has played a trick on you. Many evolutionists are keen to explain that belief in God gave primitive man an evolutionary advantage, but these same evolutionists don't think that is a good reason for advanced people like us to continue to believe in God. Similarly, if we now "know" that the notion of evil is just a useful fiction, why pretend it is real? Just grow up and face the world in all its horrendous reality – there is no evil. But this is obviously

[151] Frank Turek, *Stealing from God: Why atheists need God to make their case*, NavPress, 2014, p. 101.

wrong, and everyone knows it. Everyone knows that there are actions that are truly evil, but that moral reality cannot be accounted for by evolution.

Society

This is another common retort. I touched on it in the sample conversation above. Society sets the standards and if we want a cohesive society we get on board with those standards. However, this means that societies are by definition moral and all the moral reformers of the past were by definition immoral. We understand that a human law doesn't magically make an action good or evil; laws are intended to reflect the reality that there is good and evil. Furthermore, torturing a child for fun doesn't cease being immoral once you land on the desert island where there are no laws and where there is no society.

Human flourishing

This comeback has to do with the fact that if we all went around lying, stealing and killing then we (personally and collectively) wouldn't be very happy. If we want humanity to flourish, then it is bad to do those things. There is an objective moral duty smuggled in here at the start: that we should care about the flourishing of the human race. But of course, if atheism is true then humans have no intrinsic value. Why is anyone under any obligation to care about the flourishing of homo sapiens?

It also removes any moral quality from any action. If you have a goal, then you can assess any action as good or bad based on how well it helps you achieve the goal, but this isn't a moral goodness. If your goal is to drive a nail into a block of wood then you could say using a banana is bad, and using a hammer is good, but of course you don't mean using a banana is evil and using a hammer is virtuous. You are only thinking in terms of achieving the goal. And as we have said, the atheist's goal of human flourishing is an arbitrary goal, and atheists can only assess actions as good or bad based on how those actions contribute to that goal. A conversation I had with a woman who described herself as a militant atheist will give you an idea of what this looks like in real life. She brought up the subject of abortion. Here's how it went:

- I wouldn't ever have an abortion, but I think it should be left to a woman's own choice.

- **Why wouldn't you ever have an abortion?**

- I don't think you should kill babies.

- **I'm glad to hear that, but I don't think killing babies is something that anyone should have the "right" to do. But I'm curious, according to your view, why is killing babies wrong?**

- Of course it's wrong!

- **I agree, but you're an atheist, you believe that we are just a collection of chemicals that arrived here by a mindless process and we are heading for oblivion. That's your view – how does that lead to the conclusion, "It's wrong to kill babies"?**

- So you're saying the only reason you don't kill babies is because God told you or because you want to go to heaven? That's messed up.

- **No, you're missing the point. We both agree it's wrong to kill babies, but I can ground that in the fact that humans are made in God's image and have intrinsic value. I'm asking you, given your atheism, what is wrong with killing babies?**

- Well, if everyone killed babies then there would be no human race. We have to protect life to protect the species.

- **Right, and this is the moral bankruptcy of atheism – the only thing that's wrong with killing children is that it has a detrimental effect on others. Killing a child isn't a moral abomination, it's just not wise – that's all atheism allows you to say. Yet you know that the wanton slaughter of a child isn't just a silly thing to do, it's objectively evil.**

The Bible tells us that God has created us with the work of His law written on our hearts (Rom. 2:15). Conscience is our ally. When people hear about an elderly person being brutally beaten or a child being savagely abused, they don't just shake their heads and say the perpetrator needs to be educated. In their hearts they know the perpetrator needs to be punished (Rom. 1:32). What was done was not mentally wrong, it was morally wrong.

These three responses – evolution, society, and human

flourishing – are the go-to responses for people who want to affirm the reality of evil but deny the reality of God, and none of them works. This is why it is so important that whenever you are confronted with the reality of evil as an argument against God, you use it as a proof of God. Remember this little syllogism:

- *If a righteous God did not exist, evil would not exist;*
- *Evil does exist;*
- *Therefore, a righteous God exists.*

We have seen that a) is true – only the existence of a righteous God who imposes moral duties upon His creatures can account for how there can be such a thing as evil. And b) is certainly true – that is why the person has raised the objection against God. Therefore c) is true, a righteous God exists.

This leads to the second main point.

Look onward

There is evil in the world, and rejecting God doesn't make that evil go away; it just robs us of any hope of ultimate justice and judgment. The Bible anticipated the increase of blatant rebellion against God and violence towards man (2 Tim. 3:1-5) and assures us that God "has appointed a day on which He will judge the world in righteousness ..." (Acts 17:31). The evil dictators, child-abusers, murderers and rapists are not getting away with anything. The Bible says they are treasuring up wrath for the day of wrath (Rom. 2:5). Every day they live, and every sin they commit, increases and intensifies the load of judgment which they will receive.

This brings us to our third point.

Look inward

As you tell someone that evil is going to be judged, you will get the question, "What is He waiting for?" Why does God's judgment tarry as evil abounds? It is at this point you want to make things personal and challenging. Here's what I mean:

- Why does God allow all this wickedness in the world? Why doesn't He stop it?

- **Well, He will. The Bible says He has appointed a day in which He will judge the world.**

- But why doesn't He do it now? Why does He allow all this to continue?

- **Right, so you want God's judgment to start, but where do you want it to stop?**

- What do you mean?

- **What I mean is this – you want God to judge all the bad people, but have you ever done anything bad?**

- Of course I have, but not like them.

- **Right, so you want God to punish the people who commit sins you can't tolerate, but draw the line** at people who commit sins you can tolerate. The thing is, God can't tolerate any sin, and when He judges, He will judge in righteousness, which means that everyone who has broken His law will be punished. That is why God hasn't moved in judgment yet – He is giving people an opportunity to take the provision of salvation He has made. The Bible says He is longsuffering toward us, not willing that any should perish, but that all should come to repentance. We all ought to be very relieved that God is not swift to judge or we all would be condemned.

The fact of evil in the world shows the necessity of God's existence, but when you press home the fact of evil in an individual's life it shows the necessity of God's salvation. So you don't need to be on the defensive when it comes to the problem of moral evil, you can go on the offensive with it and use it to get to the reality of God, guilt, and grace.

Natural Evil

This is to do with why God would allow all the suffering in the world that is not the direct result of anyone's actions, like earthquakes, tsunamis, famines, and diseases.

You can answer this question in one of two ways, and it is important that you choose the right option. Some people who ask the question are coming at it *intellectually*. They are standing on the sidelines, so to speak, and, looking at all the suffering, they wonder why a good God would allow that. But others are approaching the question *emotionally*. They have just lost a child, or been diagnosed with a terminal illness, or any number of other things; they spend their lives in pain. They can't escape the sorrow this world has dumped on their lap and they are crying out an anguished, "Why?"

It is crucial to discern whether the person needs an answer for the mind or for the heart. If you start giving comfort to someone who is just wondering about the matter, then he may well think Christianity doesn't have real answers to the real issues. However, if you start explaining why it is morally permissible for God to allow suffering to someone whose heart is breaking you will come across as callous and cold.

Sometimes it is best to ask, "Before I try to answer, I'm just curious if there's anything behind your question I should know about? Has something happened in your life that has led you to think about this, or are you just wondering?"[152]

Let's look now at how we could respond to this challenge.

The problem raised intellectually

A preliminary thing to point out is that even if you can't account for why God would allow suffering in the world, that doesn't remove all the positive evidence for His existence. The scriptural and scientific proofs we have looked at don't disappear at the sight of suffering. It is

---

[152.] When we have encountered people in deep sorrow, we have found it useful to offer to pray for them then and there. It not only communicates that you care; it communicates that you believe that God cares.

entirely legitimate then, if you have presented evidence for the God of scripture, to say to someone who raises the question of suffering merely as a debating point, "You are changing the subject. That's a good question, but do you see that it doesn't address the evidence I have given you?"

The suffering around us leads many to doubt that there is a good and powerful God, but creation shows there is a powerful God, and conscience shows He is a good God. The suffering in the world ought to make us ask what has gone wrong rather than think God doesn't exist.

John Lennox has made this point by saying that when we see a building that has been bombed, we don't conclude that no one designed or made the building. Indeed, sometimes the evidence of design can become more apparent as we look at the bombed remains. The proper response to seeing a bombed building is not to conclude no one made it, it is to ask, "What happened?"

The suffering in our world strikes us as a problem precisely because we recognise things shouldn't be this way. We have a sense that something has gone wrong, but this intuition makes no sense on an atheistic (or any other non-Biblical) view of the world. If there is no way things ought to be, then why would we ever have the idea that there is?

So suffering isn't a good reason to believe there is no God, but the challenge does remain – why would the God of the Bible allow all this suffering in the world? That is an entirely fair question, and one that the Bible doesn't dodge.

Why did it start?

If God created the world and it was good, then why does it seem far from good now? The answer is found in what we call the Fall. The first man, Adam, was made head of creation. Adam was distinct from what had previously been created – he had freedom to make choices and enjoy friendship with God. While he was rightly related to God, he was rightly related to all of creation. Everything was as it should be. When he sinned, his rebellion affected the entire creation. The world was damaged. The suffering we see is a continual reminder that something has gone wrong.

But did God not know that man was going to rebel and usher in all this sorrow and grief? He knew it full well. So why then did He go ahead with the plan? Why not just scrap it? Because scrapping His plan lets evil win. God wouldn't let evil stop His good plan of creation, nor would He let it spoil His plan – He had the answer ready.

Why hasn't it stopped?

Why has God not moved in to stop this suffering? Well, in a sense He did. When the Lord Jesus was here He performed what the Bible calls "the powers of the age to come" (Heb. 6:5). By His miracles, He was giving people a preview of what the world will be like under His reign. He healed the sick, calmed the storm, and fed the hungry, so when He reigns there will be no sickness, no natural disasters, and no famine. But He was rejected. The people would not bow to His authority, in fact they had Him crucified, crying, "We have no king but Caesar" (John 19:15). We can't have the blessings of Christ's reign without having His reign, so those blessings are not enjoyed in this age. They will be enjoyed in the age to come, when He returns to take His rightful place as King.

So, why does He not just come and set up His Kingdom? The reason is that He wants sinners to bow to His authority now so that they can enjoy that glorious future free from all the effects of sin. In the meantime, we remain in a ragged world. The King is absent, the revolt continues, and when He comes the rebels will be exiled. In longsuffering, He sends His ambassadors to urge sinners, "Be reconciled to God" (2 Cor. 5:20).

Meanwhile, God has a good purpose in allowing what He allows. It is not God's intention to treat us like pets and merely make us happy. Some honest reflection shows that suffering can produce very worthwhile results.

First, *it breaks us down.* Suffering exposes our frailty and mortality. It shows us that we aren't here to stay, and it can bring eternity sharply into focus when otherwise it would have been out of sight and out of mind. Many proud, successful, and supposedly self-sufficient people have been brought to their knees in repentance before God through a trial which He has permitted in their life. The infliction of temporary pain has yielded an immeasurable and eternal good. The fact that the gospel is prospering in countries where suffering is more widely and deeply felt than in first-world countries shows that suffering more often than not drives people to God rather than drives them away from Him.[153] As C. S. Lewis said, "God whispers to us in our pleasures, speaks in our consciences, but shouts in our pains. It is His megaphone to rouse a deaf world."[154]

Secondly, *it builds us up*. I think most of us would acknowledge that we would be very shallow, silly, and spoilt individuals if we had never faced any adversity in life. Parents who mollycoddle their son up into adolescence and shield him from all disappointment and discipline are producing a brat, not a mature and useful man. Similarly, God isn't going to shield us from all the trials and horrors of living in a fallen world. His goal is not our happiness but our good. The greatest good (and deepest joy) for humanity is knowing God, and suffering often contributes to that end. As Paul said, "we glory in tribulations also: knowing that tribulation worketh patience; and patience, experience; and experience, hope ..." (Rom. 5:3-4, KJV).

So the problem of why a good God would allow suffering can be answered intellectually, but often that's not the angle from which people are approaching this subject. That's why we also need to consider a response aimed at the emotions.

The problem raised emotionally

You may encounter someone whose question is not, "Why would God allow so much suffering in the world?", but rather it is, "Why would God allow so much suffering in my life?"

[153.] See *Global Christianity: A Report on the Size and Distribution of the World's Christian Population* by the Pew Forum on Religion & Public Life, December 2011, http://www.pewforum.org/files/2011/12/Christianity-fullreport-web.pdf.
[154.] C. S. Lewis, *The Problem of Pain*, HarperCollins, 1996, p. 91.

The little slogan, "People don't care how much you know until they know how much you care," is useful to keep in mind when you speak to people in difficult circumstances. You need to communicate that you care and that God cares. Don't rush in with answers. Job's friends were good comforters until they began to tell Job why he was in the mess he was in.

While in many scenarios it is appropriate to communicate certainty, that is not the case here. I often illustrate the point by saying something like this:

It should really come as no surprise that we can't understand God's reasons for everything He allows. When our children were small, my wife took them to someone who stabbed them with a needle, and it hurt. There was no point in my wife beginning to explain to them that this vaccination that the nurse gave would prevent them getting diseases in the future. They didn't have the mental capacity at that time to take that information in. It was impossible for them to understand why their mum would allow, or even cause, them to suffer in this way when she could have prevented it. But when they were crying they didn't turn away from their mum, they turned to her in their pain, because they had enough evidence and experience in their little lives to know that she loved them and could be trusted.

Now, if we can accept that the gap between the intellect of God and us is far greater than the gap between the intellect of a mother and child, then it is obvious that there are going to be

*things God allows that we can't understand yet, and it would
be futile for God to explain the reasons to us. The question
is, do we have evidence that God loves us? And the answer to
that is yes.*

The atheistic philosopher, Bertrand Russell, is supposed
to have asked what Christians could say at the bedside
of a dying child. It's a good question, but here's another
– what does the atheist have to say at the bedside of a
dying child? At least the Christian has something to say
in the face of tragedy – there is a God of love and there is
a reason to hope.

The evidence of God's love is seen in the cross. This
is what assured Paul of God's love in the midst of his
sufferings (Rom. 5:5-8). Even if we can't understand the
reason for our pain, we can see the reason for Christ's pain
– "Christ died for us." Love that would go so far and give
so much is love that will never die. In the shadow of the
cross we are assured that God hasn't abandoned this world
– He loves us.

*If we again ask the question: 'Why does God allow evil and
suffering to continue?' and we look at the cross of Jesus, we
still do not know what the answer is. However, we now know
what the answer isn't. It can't be that he doesn't love us.*[155]

[155.] Timothy Keller, *The Reason for God: Belief in an Age of Scepticism*,
Hodder & Stoughton, 2008, p. 30.

Furthermore, in light of the empty tomb we are assured there is hope. The resurrection of the Lord Jesus from the dead shows that suffering and death will not have the last word. For those linked with Christ there is a glorious future where death is conquered and suffering is gone. Looking at suffering through resurrection glasses, Paul said, "For our light affliction, which is but for a moment, worketh for us a far more exceeding and eternal weight of glory" (2 Cor. 4:17, KJV).

This is not wishful thinking or mere optimism. As we will see later, Jesus is the Son of God, so His death is the supreme demonstration of God's love, and He rose from the dead, so there is real hope.

Conclusion

The problem of why God allows evil and suffering is one that can't be answered in a sound bite, but if you have someone who is serious and wants answers, then the Bible has them – answers that address the intellect and emotions in a satisfying way. And this huge challenge can be more than merely answered; it can be used as a means of proving the God of scripture and advancing the gospel.[156]

[156.] Notice that in addressing the problem of moral evil we have been drawing on Romans 2, and in addressing the problem of natural evil we have been mainly in Romans 5 (the first 11 verses address the emotional problem, the concluding verses the intellectual problem). This shows the importance of having a grasp of this epistle if we are not only to declare the gospel clearly but defend it convincingly.

Chapter 10

SALVATION

I don't think it's fair that all the good people from all the other religions go to hell just because they don't believe in Jesus.

Our society is becoming increasingly intolerant of people who think that they are right and everyone else is wrong. They say that dogmatism and certainty lead to division and exclusion.[157] What, in their view, could be more arrogant than the claim to know who goes to heaven and who doesn't? What could be more intolerant than saying that only people in your group are accepted by God? What could be more psychologically damaging than telling people they are going to hell forever?

In this chapter we are going to look at some of the objections to the Christian view of salvation and see how we can respond in a way that shows that the Biblical way of salvation makes sense.

[157.] It seems lost on them that they make these claims dogmatically and with great certainty.

1. The narrow way is narrow minded

Christ is essential for salvation

I was travelling with a former colleague (Phil) to a work-related event. It was a long journey and we had plenty of time to chat, so he told me about a trip he had taken to Guinea to do some building work. He told me he had been staying with an American missionary couple. Phil wasn't a Christian, and I was interested in how he got on staying with Christian missionaries.

"They were very nice and looked after me well," he said, "but you do have to wonder what they're doing there."

"Why's that?" I asked.

"Well, it seems to me that the people there are as upright as people in America, so it just seems a bit arrogant for these Americans to come over to Guinea and say, 'You have to change your beliefs for our beliefs, and if you don't, you'll go to hell.'"

And Phil was right, wasn't he? The way he stated it does make those missionaries seem arrogant and God seem petty. After all, surely God is more concerned with how people behave than what they believe, isn't He? He wouldn't disqualify someone from heaven for not dotting their theological i's or crossing their theological t's, would He?

Are all other religions excluded from heaven because their doctrine is wrong? Was Christ being arrogant when He said, "I am the way"? Were His apostles bigoted when they said, "Neither is there salvation in any other ..."? Are

Christians today narrow-minded when they say that those who don't believe in Christ are lost?

This is a subject where it is very easy to give the right answer but leave the wrong impression. Someone asks, "Are you saying that no matter how good I am, if I don't receive Christ I am going to hell?" If we say, "Yes," we have answered accurately, but not adequately. We have answered the question, but not the questioner because the person asking the question isn't just looking for an answer but a reason. We need to tell people not only *that* they need Christ, but *why* they need Christ.

Greg Koukl has illustrated the problem this way:[158] people think the Christian message is that God looks down from heaven on all the different religions of the world and He picks His favourite. His favourite is Christianity, and all the others can, quite literally, go to hell. If that were a true representation of the gospel then it would present a very unfair God, but that is not the biblical gospel. God doesn't pick His favourite religious group. It is rather that He sees everyone, whatever their religious label, as a sinner, guilty of breaking His law and deserving of His judgment. He has provided the answer to their sin in the sacrifice of Christ, and is offering Christ to sinners as a Saviour and substitute. Refusing the Saviour doesn't *put* you in danger, it *keeps* you there. If you reject the substitute there's no other option, you take the punishment yourself.

Look at it another way. Imagine yourself on a cruise ship

---

158. https://www.youtube.com/watch?v=s6zpySZDBo0&sns=em.

and the captain comes to you holding a lifebelt. He tells you he wants you to take the lifebelt. When you ask why, he tells you that the lifebelt is very precious to him and he wants you to take it or he will throw you overboard. At this point you might almost prefer to be overboard than on a cruise with a captain who is so petty and cruel. But many people understand the gospel in this way. They think God is saying to us, "My Son is precious to Me, and if you don't accept Him I will be so cross I will throw you into hell." So people are condemned to hell just because they didn't accept Christ.

Let's change the picture to make it more accurate. You are on the cruise ship, but through your own foolishness and flouting of the rules you fall overboard. The captain throws out the lifeline to you and it lands within your reach. When you are gasping for breath and taking in water, unable to keep afloat, the necessity of grasping the lifebelt makes perfect sense. If someone refuses it, he is refusing the only means of salvation. The cause of death isn't "rejected lifebelt". The cause of death is drowning. The lifebelt was the answer to the problem, not the cause of it. What we want to do therefore is help people understand the nature of their problem and then they will see the reason why Christ is the only answer.

So, as counterintuitive as it seems, don't be too quick to give people the good news. We need to close off every self-righteous avenue of escape from condemnation, and show that because God is righteous there is no hope for the guilty outside of Christ.

It was this thought of God's righteousness that tormented Martin Luther and made him realise he could never merit salvation. He said he hated the words, "the righteousness of God." They were a thunderbolt to his heart and struck his conscience like lightning. He had fallen short of God's righteous demands and thus justice demanded his condemnation, no matter how good he was or how hard he tried. Works-based, man-made religion was useless. He was lost.

If people see the problem, then they will be glad to hear about the answer. When, like Luther, we learn that God is righteous, then the emptiness of religion and the exclusivity of salvation through Christ make perfect sense.

Mankind faces a singular problem. People are broken and the world is broken because our friendship with God has been broken, ruined by human rebellion. Humans, you and I – are guilty, enslaved, lost, dead. All of us. Everyone. Everywhere. The guilt must be punished, the debt must be paid, the slave must be purchased. Promising better conduct in the future will not mend the crimes of the past. No, a rescuer must ransom the slaves, a kindred brother must pay the family debt, a substitute must shoulder the guilt. There is no other way of escape.

This is why Jesus of Nazareth is the only way to God, the only possible source of rescue. He is the only one who solved the problem. No other man did this. No other person could. Not Mohammed. Not the Buddha. Not Krishna. Not anyone else.

Only Jesus of Nazareth could save the world. Without him we are crushed under our overwhelming debt. Without him, every single one of us would have to pay for our own crimes, and that would take eternity.[159]

It's not a matter then that God throws people into hell because they failed the cosmic Religious Education exam. People need the Lord the same way a debtor needs a wealthy and generous friend. Many could offer sympathy and financial advice to a man deeply in debt. What he needs, however, is money. Similarly, religions may be able to give us good advice on how to live fulfilling lives, and help us get on well with our neighbour, but what we need is an answer to our guilt, a Saviour from our sin, a payment for our debt, and that can only be found in Christ.

I was speaking with a couple of Muslim men, and I told them I had been reading through the Koran and I had some questions. I told them that one of the things I noticed in the Koran was the insistence on Allah being righteous. They agreed that this was true. But another theme throughout the Koran is that he is all-merciful. Again, they agreed. "My problem is this," I said, "I can't see how both of those things can be true. How can he be righteous and merciful? If he's righteous he punishes sin, but if he's merciful then he lets the sinner go free."

They acknowledged that was a puzzle that they hadn't really thought about before, so we explored some potential

---

[159.] Gregory Koukl, *The Story of Reality*, p. 132.

solutions and agreed that they didn't really work. After all our efforts to reconcile these attributes in Allah failed, they said to me, "But you're a Christian. You believe God is righteous and merciful, so you have the same problem." It was great to be able to tell them that the Christian message has the answer – the cross.

This led to a golden opportunity to point them to the sacrifice of Christ as the solution to the question mankind has always asked and religion has never answered – how can a righteous God forgive sins? Or as Job put it (Job 9:2), "How can a man be righteous before God?"

Christ is enough for salvation

When you speak to people from other religious backgrounds you will have to try to help them see that the cross of Christ is *necessary* for their salvation, but when you talk to someone from a nominally Christian background you will have to emphasise that it is *sufficient* for their salvation. The vast majority of church attendees believe that their salvation in some way depends on their performance; whether it is a Catholic, a cultist, or just your typical church member, they think that they have to earn God's acceptance. Often they will disclaim any notion that they can merit salvation. They will tell you that they are depending on God's strength and they aren't good enough and they need His grace, but the problem is that they believe that, even though they aren't perfect, they have to try hard enough to get God's grace and benefit from Christ's blood. They can live lives so bad that the grace of God won't reach them and the blood of Christ can't cleanse them. If God's grace and strength are available for all, but only some live a good enough life, where does the difference lie? The difference lies in the people living the life – they have done better and tried harder, thus they have earned their salvation – something the Bible says is impossible (Rom. 3:27; 4:2-3; Eph. 2:8-9).

A sample conversation with a "Jehovah's Witness" (Norman) will illustrate the point:[160]

- **Hello. My name is Paul. I see you are giving out literature about the Bible. I was reading the book of Romans, and I would be interested to know your view on the subject of justification in that book.**

- What do you mean?

- **Well, Romans is all about the good news of the gospel, so I assume you are familiar with it, and Paul talks a lot about how we can be justified before God.**

- Well, I think God looks at the whole of our lives and if we have tried hard enough to please Him then, even though we aren't perfect, He will justify us.

- **Okay, so you think justification is something we get in the future and it depends on whether we've tried hard enough?**

[160.] I have picked a Jehovah's Witness, but this approach is applicable to any group that claims the Bible as their authority yet believes that works are required for salvation.

- Yes. What's your view?

- Well, I have a couple of problems with what you have said. First of all, when Paul speaks about people being justified he does it in the past tense. Look at 5:1: "Therefore, having been justified by faith, we have peace with God..." This was something that Paul and the people to whom he wrote already had. They weren't waiting for it. And the other issue is that Paul says that our efforts play no part in it. Look at 4:5: "But to him who does not work but believes on Him who justifies the ungodly, his faith is accounted for righteousness".

- So you're saying that it doesn't matter how you live?

- At this stage, all I'm doing is showing you what Paul wrote, and he said that justification is "to him who does not work but believes..."

- So you can live just whatever way you want then? You can murder and steal and lie and it doesn't matter?

- I'm really glad you asked that, because that is the very question Paul expected someone to ask. In 6:1 he anticipates the objection you have raised when he says, "Shall we continue in sin that grace may abound?" Can you see, Norman, that if the message of justification was that we had to keep trying, then there is no way anyone would have raised this question?

- Well, the Bible does say that we are to work out our own salvation with fear and trembling.

- **Okay, but let's not move away from Romans just yet. We can come back to that later if you want. The question Paul anticipates wouldn't be asked if our works played a part in justification. And look, Paul's answer isn't to say, "No, you will lose your justification if you do that." His answer is that the Christian has been set free from the grip of sin – we are no longer enslaved to it. Why then would we ever want to continue in its service? When the Lord saved me, He gave me His Holy Spirit. He has given me new life, and new desires.[161]**

To put it in its most simple terms, the difference between the message of the gospel and the messages of religion is that the gospel offers a Saviour. The religions of the world have gurus and prophets who tell us how to live, but none of them claimed to be able to save. When people realise they are condemned and can't earn God's acceptance, then the message of salvation through Christ alone no longer sounds arrogant.

After I tried explaining this to Phil on our journey I asked him what he thought. He said it helped him understand the missionaries' motivation better. He then said, "I think I had better tell you this – while I was there, the chief of

---

[161.] For more on this see Paul McCauley, *He that believeth: Establishing the Truth of Eternal Security*, John Ritchie Ltd, 2015, pp. 37-39, 129-148.

one of the tribes came to the missionaries I was staying with and said, 'Why has it taken you so long to bring us this message?'" Those people saw that the Christian gospel offered something their religion didn't, something they desperately needed – a Saviour.

2. What about those who have never heard?

The question of that chief in Guinea leads to the question, what about those who have never heard about Christ?

We need to keep in mind why people need Christ – it is because they have sinned and deserve punishment. Even without access to a Bible, people know that there is a God to whom they are accountable. This God has given mankind a conscience and written the work of the law on the hearts of all (Rom. 1:18-32; 2:15). So when people sin, they do it against a known law and are justly condemned. This means that hearing about Christ is an act of grace, not a matter of fairness. Prison is for those who break the law, and there is no obligation for any criminal to be offered a pardon. Therefore the person who has never heard of Christ has no just cause for complaint – he will get what he deserves, nothing more. That is why Christ gave the Great Commission. People need to hear the gospel – they have no hope of escaping their just punishment apart from Christ.

But remember, God has many ways of getting the gospel to those who are seeking. If someone in an unreached tribe in a remote village responds to the light he has (i.e. that he has sinned against God) and is seeking God, then God will get the message of salvation to him.

In Death of a Guru, Rabindranath Maharaj tells his story. Rabi was a young Yogi, a Guru and a member of the Brahman caste. He'd experienced astral travel to other planets, had psychedelic experiences, and received yogic visions. Deep meditation led to higher and higher states of consciousness.

Rabi discovered, though, that each step closer to his Hindu gods was a step farther from the true God he sought in his heart. When confronted with the utter emptiness of life and the shallowness of religion, he cried out, "I want to know the true God, the Creator of the universe!" God responded by bringing the Gospel to him through the witness of a young woman named Molli.[162]

And we have scriptural examples of this. In Acts 8 and 10 we have examples of how God moves heaven and earth to get the gospel to seeking sinners. In both of these chapters there is angelic activity as well as human agency involved. In Acts 8 the angel directs the Christian to the seeker, while in Acts 10 he directs the seeker to the Christian. So we can have confidence that no one seeking the light will be left in the dark.[163]

3. Hitler and Grandma

It's something that many upright, respectable people just can't understand. No matter how bad that person is, he

---

[162] https://www.str.org/publications/is-jesus-the-only-way#.WWUvx9QrKt8, referring to Rabindranath R. Maharaj, *Death of a Guru*, A. J. Holman, 1977.

[163] Especially when we consider that the only reason anyone seeks God is because of a work of God in the heart (Rom. 3:11; John 6:44).

can go to heaven if he prays a prayer, and no matter how good I am, I go to hell if I don't pray the prayer? That seems unfair. Is it true then that Hitler could have gone to heaven after all the evil that he did, and someone's sweet old grandmother could go to hell after all the good that she did? What we have looked at already should help us in addressing this objection.

When confronted with the Hitler objection, keep the following points in mind. First, salvation is not found in praying a prayer but in repentance and faith. Someone can say he has repented, but God knows. Secondly, sin has a hardening effect. People who do what Hitler did have rejected a lot of God-given light and beaten their conscience to death, so it would be very unusual that after years of justifying evil someone would change his attitude and desire forgiveness. As others have said, true repentance is never too late, but late repentance is rarely true. Thirdly, if someone repents, then he will be prepared to face the consequences of his actions and want to do what he can, so far as possible, to put right what he has done wrong, rather than try to escape it through suicide.[164]

That said, *if* Hitler had repented, that is, agreed with God about his sin, recognising it as hateful and hell-deserving, and turned to Christ for forgiveness, then such is the vastness of God's grace and the value of Christ's blood that his sins would have been forgiven. Our grace wouldn't

---

[164.] That is not at all meant to imply that someone committing suicide means he or she wasn't saved. Sometimes mental illness or the sheer burden of guilt has led people to end their lives. Needless to say, there is no evidence that Hitler's suicide was motivated by anything other than selfishness and cowardice.

extend that far, but that's why God's grace is amazing. It doesn't minimise the seriousness of the atrocities he committed – the gospel affirms that it took nothing less than the sacrifice of God's Son to pay for those crimes. History shows that the lowest, worst, hardest, and vilest can be and have been saved. From the malefactor crucified beside Christ to Saul of Tarsus, the chief of sinners, to John Newton, the blasphemous slave trader, to Mitsuo Fuchida, the man who led the assault on Pearl Harbour, example after example can be given of those who have been guilty of heinous crimes finding soul-cleansing forgiveness and life-changing power in Christ, proving the truth of what the Bible says, "He is ... able to save" (Heb. 7:25).

Now what about the sweet grandmother? If she has never sinned then she doesn't have to worry about going to hell. Hell is the place where people are punished for their sins. No sins, no punishment. However, if Grandma has sinned (and of course she has) then she needs Christ. Her sins can't be glossed over – the account has to be settled. If she accepts the provision for her sin she will be saved, if she doesn't she won't.

Justice demands the condemnation of all outside of Christ. But justice also demands the justification of all in Christ.

4. Hell, too bad to be true?

The thought of hell is deeply troubling. It's meant to be. But is there such a place? And what kind of a God would punish people forever for sins committed in a few years?

The Bible teaches the reality of eternal conscious punishment.[165] The problem people have is that it seems like a cosmic overreaction. People don't feel like their sins deserve that. If you encounter this objection, keep the following things in mind:[166]

a) The inerrant nature of scripture

If the Bible is God's word and it teaches we deserve hell, then it is right and we are wrong, regardless of how we feel. Bring the authority of scripture to bear on the issue (using the arguments of chapter 7).

b) The infinite holiness of God

God is infinitely holy and sin-hating. Every sin defies His authority and defaces His image. He has created us in His image, as His representatives, and when we sin we demean Him. "Hell is God's declaration to the universe that what every sin demeans is of infinite worth."[167] To sin against Him is to seek to dethrone Him. We are putting ourselves in His place, and thus committing a crime of infinite seriousness which carries with it an infinite penalty. That is why the punishment lasts forever – as finite creatures we can never pay an infinite penalty. As one Bible teacher

---

[165.] See Paul McCauley, *He that believeth not.*

[166.] As well as what was considered in chapter 3.

[167.] John Piper, *Jesus: The Only Way to God – Must You Hear the Gospel to be Saved?*, Baker Books, 2010, p. 32.

put it, "Sin is an offence against the infinitely holy God. Its gravity cannot be computed. The supreme dignity of the One against whom man has sinned makes his wrongdoing infinite in gravity."[168]

c) The intrinsic value of humanity

God has invested mankind with intrinsic worth, and He will not therefore snuff them out of existence because they have rebelled against Him. If they don't want God, then they will be exiled from Him, but not extinguished by Him.

Conclusion

The gospel really is good news, but there are clouds of confusion that need to be cleared away before people can see its light and feel its warmth. The "bigotry" of supposing that your way is the only way is not bigotry at all; the gospel is the only message that even professes to offer what we need – a Saviour. Since it is a Saviour that we need then it makes no sense to talk about the unevangelised being treated unfairly. They will be treated fairly – that's the problem, and that's why they need to hear about Christ. The amazing grace of God is offensive to the proud, but God is perfectly righteous in saving the repentant, no matter how bad they are, and God is perfectly righteous in condemning the unrepentant, no matter how good they are. The truth of eternal punishment seems extreme until we realise that

---

[168.] E. W. Rogers, *Treasury of Bible Doctrine*, Precious Seed Publications, 1977, pp. 432-433.

God's hatred of sin cannot be limited. The punishment must be infinite, and therefore for finite creatures it must be eternal.

If people are prepared to listen, and you are prepared with answers, you can help them, in God's power, to see how good and glorious the gospel of the glory of the blessed God really is.

Chapter 11

THE SAVIOUR

*There is as much evidence for Thor being the son of Odin as
there is for Jesus being the Son of God.*

Jesus Christ is the most influential and controversial figure
in all of history. It seems that almost every religion and
cause wants to have Him on their side, but in a modified
version. Everyone wants Him, but not as He is. So He is not
only the most attractive person ever, but the most attacked.
Every Christmas and Easter, some major publication will
carry an exclusive story about Jesus that claims something
scandalous; something which, if true, spells the end of
orthodox Christianity. Unfortunately the smoke from these
firestorms lingers on the internet long after the fire has been
put out by the facts.

There are four fundamentals of the faith relating to Christ
– His humanity, His deity, His death, and His resurrection.
These four truths form the *sine qua non* of the gospel. If any
one of them is denied, the denier is not a Christian; if any

one of them is false, then Christianity is false. You can see the importance of these truths in relation to salvation in that well-known gospel verse, Romans 10:9:

> because, if you confess with your mouth that Jesus is Lord and believe in your heart that God raised him from the dead, you will be saved. (ESV)

Salvation involves a confession that Jesus (His humanity) is Lord (His deity), and believing that God raised Him (His resurrection) from the dead (His death). Given the fundamental importance of these truths, it is vital that we can defend them against attack and present a positive case for them.

1. The humanity of Christ

In this section, we won't be defending the fact that the Lord Jesus possessed true humanity because that is something we have never had to defend in our evangelism. We will be giving a defence of the historicity of Christ, because unfortunately we do come across this from time to time.

The existence of Jesus of Nazareth is something that is beyond any serious dispute, and deniers of it tend to lurk on the internet far away from the reach of responsible scholarship. Usually, when we come across someone who denies the existence of Jesus, our first port of call is not to take their objection seriously. We would respond with something like, "Well, there's no doubt He existed. Almost everyone who knows anything about history knows that

He existed. The question is, 'Is He who He claimed to be?'" Usually this is enough to get the issue of His existence off the table and allow you to present a case for His deity.

If they persist in denying His existence, then ask them to give an account of why they would do that. Say to them, "I'm curious, almost every scholar of ancient history, whether Christian or atheist, believes Jesus existed. What do you know that they don't?" Make them shoulder the responsibility of defending the claim they have made. They will perhaps come back with something vague like, "There's no evidence." Ask them what they mean. Ask them what they know about the writings we have from the first century that speak about Jesus.

Every person we have met who has issued this challenge has the idea they have nothing to prove – you are the one making the claim, so you are the one that bears the burden. Now that rule ("whoever makes the claim bears the burden") is a good rule, but all you have to do is say, "We have loads of evidence from the first century that comes from those who knew Jesus. How do you know it's all false?" Now he is making a claim – "All those documents are false," so now he bears the burden – why would he say they are false, what reasons does he have? Let's see how this might look in conversation.

- **Hello, we are just giving out some booklets here about the relevance of Jesus Christ. Would you be interested in that?**
- No. I don't believe any of that.

- **Oh. Why is that?**

- There's no evidence Jesus ever existed.

- **No evidence He ever existed?! Are you serious?**

- Yes!

- **Are you a historian?**

- No.

- **Well, those who are historians agree that there's loads of evidence for the existence of Jesus.**

- Yes, but they're all Christians, so of course they would say that.

- **Well, that's just not true. There are many New Testament scholars and ancient historians who are not at all sympathetic to Christianity, but they believe Jesus existed.**

- But there's no proof.

- **What do you mean?**

- There's only what was written in the Bible years later.

- **What do you know about the New Testament documents?**

- Well, I know that they weren't written by the people they say they were written by; they were written decades and decades later.

- **How do you know that?**

- There was this thing on Discovery Channel a few months ago.

- **What was that?**

- They were showing that the Gospels were political documents to get power.

- **How did they show that?**

- Well, I can't remember all the details now.

- **Did you check out those claims or investigate any responses or other points of view?**

- Well, no.

- **Would that be an example of blind faith?**

- What?

- **If I told you I believed the Bible just because some smart person told me it was true, I think you would be less than impressed and not at all convinced. That's what's going on here – you are telling me what someone has told you and you haven't investigated it for yourself.**

Once you have cleared away all the bluster, and you have someone who is genuinely interested in knowing what the evidence is for the existence of Jesus, then you can make a positive case.

Historians have a number of criteria they use to establish the historicity of a person or event, and all these criteria are met by Jesus. Consider the following examples:

We have early testimonies[169]

The Gospels were all written within the lifetime of people who would have witnessed the events, and three of the four Gospels (Matthew, Mark, and Luke) were written within 30 years of the alleged events.[170] We have the epistles of Paul in which he refers to the apostles and his personal acquaintance with them (e.g. Gal. 1:18-19; 2:1-10), and these epistles were written about 20-30 years after the events were supposed to have taken place. But even more significantly, we have within the writings of Paul examples of confessions (e.g. 1 Cor. 8:6), hymns (e.g. Php. 2:5-11), and prayers (e.g. 1 Cor. 16:22) that were in common usage amongst the Christians, and therefore predate his writings by a considerable period. Of particular significance is a creedal statement found in 1 Corinthians 15:3-8 which, scholars agree, Paul received when he met Peter and James, the Lord's brother (referred to in Gal. 1:18-19) within five years of the death of Christ.[171]

---

[169] See Norman L. Geisler & Frank Turek, *I Don't Have Enough Faith to Be an Atheist*, Crossway, 2004, pp. 221-249.

[170] This is based on the view that Luke finished writing Acts at the time Paul was under house arrest in Rome in the early 60s (why else would he not have included the details about Paul meeting Nero?), and Luke's Gospel was written before that, and Matthew and Mark were written before that. Also, 1 Timothy 5:18 quotes Luke's Gospel as scripture. 1 Timothy was written about AD 63. Obviously Luke's Gospel must have been written well before that and been circulating amongst the Christians for Paul to quote it as he did.

[171] Notice Paul does not say in 1 Corinthians 15:3 what he says in 11:23 – that he received it from the Lord. He received the gospel directly from the Lord (Gal. 1:11-12), but this creedal formula with the details of the appearances was probably received from Peter and James (Gal. 1:18-19).

We have exclusive testimonies

That is, we have multiple independent accounts for the life of Jesus. New Testament scholars point out that the information in the Gospels does not come from a single source. In addition to the information in the Gospels, we have information from the Acts and the epistles of the New Testament, as well as sources outside the Bible, such as Josephus, Tacitus, and Pliny the Younger. All these independent sources are talking about the same person and events, which is incomprehensible if He never existed.

We have eyewitness testimonies

The incidental details in the Gospel accounts, the undesigned coincidences between the Gospel accounts,[172] the use of names that accurately reflect the names of that time and place,[173] and the archaeological confirmation of the Gospel accounts all confirm that the information came from those who were on the scene. There are features that are very prominent in the Gospels that weren't prominent in the Old Testament nor in the epistles of the New Testament, and thus were obviously not Christian inventions, e.g. the designation "the Son of man", the use of the word "truly" (or "verily") at the beginning of a phrase, and the Lord's emphasis on and descriptions of hell. Also, there are details in the Gospels that would never have been imagined or invented based on the Old Testament scriptures or New

---

[172.] See especially on this, Lydia McGrew, *Hidden in Plain View: Undesigned Coincidences in the Gospels and Acts*, Deward Publishing Company Ltd, 2017.

[173.] For more on this see chapter 4 of Richard Bauckham, *Jesus and the Eyewitnesses: The Gospels as Eyewitness Testimony*, Eerdmans, 2006.

Testament doctrine, e.g. the manner in which He appeared after His resurrection.[174]

We have embarrassing testimonies

There are things that the Gospels record which are difficult to explain, or reflect badly on the apostles and make their message less likely to be believed. These things would never have been invented by the Gospel writers. They testify not only to the historicity of the events but the honesty of the authors – the events were included because they happened, and there is no attempt to explain them away. Examples of these include: the Lord's brothers not believing in Him; the cowardice and pettiness of the twelve disciples; the Lord selecting one who would betray Him; the Lord stating that He didn't know the time of His second coming; the Lord's intense agony in Gethsemane; a member of the Jewish Sanhedrin burying the Lord, while the disciples were nowhere to be seen; women being the ones who discovered His empty tomb.[175] These are just a few of the things we find in the Gospels that made the message harder to swallow – you don't make those things up.[176]

[174.] N. T. Wright points out that if a Christian were inventing resurrection appearances based on Old Testament scriptures or New Testament doctrine, he never would have come up with appearances like those recorded in the Gospels. See *The Resurrection of the Son of God*, SPCK, 2003, pp. 599-615.

[175.] This was the criticism Celsus made in his attack on Christianity, *On the True Doctrine*, written in the 170s – Christians were relying on the testimony of "a hysterical woman".

[176.] There are satisfactory explanations of these difficulties, but the point is that the text gives the difficulties and not the explanations – you don't do that if you are inventing a story you want people to believe.

We have earnest testimonies

The earnestness and integrity of the Gospel writers is seen in two ways – they were not prepared to lie, and they were prepared to die.

How can I say that they were not prepared to make up lies? Because of the things that would have been included if they were making up a story. They would have included some pronouncements of Jesus on the issues that caused problems in the early days of the church, such as circumcision, or the issues Paul addresses in 1 Corinthians 7:12, 25.[177] They would have included more explicit explanations of His deity and relationship with the Father and Spirit from His own mouth. They would have posted the guard at the tomb as soon as He had been buried rather than the next day. They would have included an account of some disciples seeing Him rise from the dead and emerge from the tomb. There are lots of things like this that would have been made up if the whole story was a fabrication and the writers had no interest in the truth.

The ultimate proof of the earnestness of the early Christians is that these people who claimed to have been with Jesus were prepared to lay down their lives for their claim. You don't suffer for something you know to be false.

For these reasons, and many others, the question of Jesus' existence is settled and the case is closed. Now, please don't be intimidated by all these points that we have made – we have included these, not for you to learn, but

---

[177.] Note how the Lord's teaching was known (1 Cor. 7:10) and Paul didn't feel free to invent commands of the Lord in verses 12 and 25.

just so you know the facts are there. You don't have to have them all memorised, but just keep one or two of the most convincing proofs in your mind that you can recall when in conversation. Here is an example of how this evidence can be used.

- **Hi there. This is a booklet about Jesus Christ. Would you be interested in reading it?**

- Not really. I mean, who knows if He even existed?

- **Oh, well, there's no reason to doubt His existence, and plenty of reasons to believe it.**

- There's about as much evidence for Jesus as there is for the existence of Thor.

- **Hmmm. What documents are there about Thor that tell you about where and when he lived, and what historical figures he interacted with? Who claimed to know Thor and was prepared to give his life for him? You see, we have absolutely no documentation that places him in real time, in real places with real people, but we have all of that when it comes to Jesus.**

- But we have nothing that Jesus ever wrote down Himself.

- **That's true, but I really don't understand what that proves. If you are saying that the whole thing is a myth that was invented by the writers of the New Testament, then why didn't they just write a** document and say that He wrote it? The reason why we don't have anything written by Him is because He didn't write anything. If they wanted to make up a story in order to get power do you not think they would pen something in His name so that it carried all His authority?

- Well, I see what you mean, but, I don't know, it just seems like a fairy tale.

- Do you mind me asking, have you read the New Testament Gospels?

- Well, not recently.

- Okay. One thing the Gospels do not resemble is a fairy tale. They refer to real places in the world and real people in history, and the people who spread the story did so at the cost of their lives. Can you think of any fairy tale like that?

- Well. I don't know. It still seems like there's a lot that was made up.

- Okay. Let me ask you this – if you were to make up a story that you wanted people to believe, would you put in details that made your story harder to believe?

- I don't know.

- You don't know? Now hold on, let's think about this, if you wanted people to believe your story, would you include things that made it harder or easier for people to believe your story?

- Well, easier.

- **Yes, of course. You wouldn't include things that made it harder for people to believe, and yet that's what we have in the Gospels. They put in details that reflect really badly on themselves, and include details that would have made people of that time dismiss their message. For example, the disciples abandoned Jesus at His arrest, none of them was there for His burial, and it was women who stood faithful to Him and found His empty tomb. In that day and culture, the testimony of a woman was deemed worthless. The only reason they would have recorded these things is because these things happened. The Gospels bear all the hallmarks of honest eyewitness testimony, not polished polemics or fancy fairy tales. There's no good reason to dispute that they are recording what happened. The question is why are you unwilling to accept their testimony?**

- Well, I'm not really that interested.

- **Okay. That was the same with me, but then I realised this is something that is relevant to me ...**

The two lines of evidence used in this conversation were earnest testimony (they weren't prepared to lie and they were prepared to die for their story), and embarrassing testimony (they include things that make their story less credible).

The denial of the historicity of Christ is something that should never come up but sadly often does. Try to communicate the foolishness of the objection in a way that doesn't make the objector look foolish. If you have one or two of the facts mentioned above at your fingertips then you should be able to deal with it quite quickly.[178]

2. The deity of Christ

Although Jesus was a real man, He was not a mere man. The Christian belief is that He was none less than God. But why should anyone believe this? There are two very simple, indisputable, and powerful points which we have found useful.

He claimed it

There is no doubt that the Lord Jesus claimed deity for Himself. Scholars who deny that the Bible is the word of God concede that Jesus repeatedly claimed divine titles and privileges, and demanded and accepted that which belongs to God alone.[179]

[178.] Something that was quite popular for a time was the view that the story of Jesus was a rehash of pagan myths of dying and rising gods. This silly argument has been decisively answered, but if you encounter it, keep the following three points in mind: first, the first Christians were Jews, they wouldn't have invented or been attracted to a story that aped the Gentile legends; second, the facts of the Gospels stand historical scrutiny whether they resemble other stories or not; third, the primary sources of these pagan myths bear no resemblance to the facts about Christ, and wherever there is a similarity the pagan source comes *after* Christ not before. For more detail see the relevant chapter in Lee Strobel, *The Case for the Real Jesus*.

[179.] Sceptical and liberal scholars concede the Lord claimed to be the unique Son of God explicitly in passages like Matt. 11:27; Mark 12:1-9; 13:32; 14:60-64. He also made implicit claims to deity by His claims of authority (e.g. Matt. 5:21-48; His use of the phrase, "Truly, I say to you"), the significance of His miracles (Luke 7:22 with Isa. 35:4-6), and His demands for supreme devotion from His followers (e.g. Matt. 10:37-39). For more on this see William Lane Craig, *On Guard, Defending Your Faith with Reason and Precision*, chapter 8.

The question then is, was He right or wrong? If He was wrong, He either thought He was right but made a mistake, or knew He was wrong and was telling lies. But neither of these two options fits the facts or is remotely possible. If He was mistaken, think of the level of delusion – He thought He was equal with God!

> *Is such an intellect – clear as the sky, bracing as the mountain air, sharp and penetrating as a sword, thoroughly healthy and vigorous, always ready and self-possessed – liable to a radical and most serious delusion concerning His own character and mission? Preposterous imagination!*[180]

If He was lying then think of the level of deception. He told people that their eternal destiny hinged on their response to Him; He called on people to follow Him no matter the cost. To make this up is wicked, and yet no one who lived the way He lived, loved the way He loved, taught the way He taught, and suffered the way He suffered could be an evil person.

We are left with no other option then – He wasn't wrong. He truly is the Son of God.

His disciples proclaimed it
It's a popular notion that the doctrine of the deity of Christ was a legendary development that reached full bloom at the Council of Nicaea. Nothing could be further from the

---

[180.] Philip Schaff, *The Person of Christ, The Perfection of His Humanity Viewed as a Proof of His Divinity*, loc 1608.

truth. As we said earlier, in the very earliest texts of the New Testament we find even earlier traditions, and these proclaim Jesus Christ as God.

This is significant because all the first Christians were Jews – they believed that there was only one God and He alone was worthy of worship, and yet these God-fearing Jews were proclaiming this crucified Nazarene to be God and worshipping Him as such. They preached Him as the one way of salvation, the fulfilment of the Covenant given through Moses, and the end of all the sacrifices. There is no way they would have dared utter such things unless there was overwhelming evidence for their truthfulness. Jesus Christ was condemned by the Sanhedrin for His claim to be God's Son, and consequently crucified by the Romans and abandoned by God. That would have extinguished any notion in the mind of a Jew that His claim was true, but God the Father vindicated Him by raising Him from the dead, and thus He was "declared to be the Son of God with power ... by the resurrection from the dead" (Rom. 1:4).

The relevance

If Jesus is the Son of God then it shows that *God has come to us*. We are not left to wonder if God is there, what He is like, or if He is interested in us. God has been revealed fully in Christ. As Rico Tice has said, "One of the great things about Jesus Christ is that when we look at him, the guessing games about God stop."[181]

[181.] Rico Tice, *Christianity Explored*.

This means that if you encounter a claim which you don't know how to counter, you can go to the authority of Christ. Here's an example:

- **Hi there. This is an invitation for some public meetings taking place to tell people about the way of salvation and how we can know we are going to heaven. Do you ever think about those things?**

- I'm a very spiritual person and I believe in reincarnation.

- **Oh right. That's interesting. Do you mind me asking, what reasons do you have to believe reincarnation is true?**

- Well, there are loads of examples of people who remember past lives that I find really convincing.

- **Okay. I have to say, I haven't really looked into that, but I have done quite a bit of study into the life of Jesus Christ, and there are two things that are firmly established historically – one is that He claimed to be the Son of God, and the second is that He didn't believe in reincarnation. So I suppose the big question is, was He right in His claim to be the Son of God? What do you think?**

- Well, I think we all are the sons and daughters of God.

- **Okay, but that certainly wasn't what Jesus was claiming. He was claiming to be the Son of God in a unique sense, in the sense that He was equal with** almighty God. In the Jewish culture in which He lived, the Jewish leaders considered His claims to be blasphemous and they wanted Him crucified for them. Jesus never said, "No, you've misunderstood – you're the sons of God too, we all are!" They knew what He was saying about Himself – He was saying He was God.

- I do think He was a great leader but I don't think He was God.

- **Well then, how can you think He was a great leader?**

- What do you mean?

- **He can't be a great leader and a great liar at the same time. He can't be a good teacher and a false teacher at the same time. If He wasn't who He claimed to be then He was either a liar or a lunatic.**

- Maybe His disciples misunderstood what He was meaning?

- **Well, all the reports we have about His life give us the same profile. And the thing is, the disciples were Jews – they believed there was only one true God and to worship anyone other than Him was blasphemy. There's no way they would have come to believe that Jesus was God unless there was overwhelming proof for it.**

- I see what you're saying, but I think everyone should have the right to their own beliefs.

- **Oh absolutely. So do I. But would you agree that when it comes to this issue it is important that we seek the truth, because if Jesus is God then when we die we won't come back as something else, but we will go to either heaven or hell?**

- Yes, but ...

Notice that the conversation never really went into the issue of reincarnation.[182] It short-circuited that topic and got straight to the person of Christ. If He is God then anyone who disagrees with Him is wrong, and any faith that contradicts Him is false.

The deity of Christ is relevant, not only in showing God has come to us, but in showing that *we can come to God.* Jesus didn't come merely to be a perfect example or a wise teacher. He came to be the great sacrifice for sin. By His death He has made it possible for man to be reconciled to God. That is our next consideration.

3. The death of Christ

Richard Dawkins asked the question, "If God wanted to forgive our sins, why not just forgive them, without having himself tortured and executed in payment ...?"[183]

[182.] The supposed evidence for reincarnation is evidence for the reality of the spiritual world and demonic deception. See, for example, the relevant chapter in Ravi Zacharias & Norman Geisler (ed.), *Who Made God? And Answers to Over 100 Other Tough Questions of Faith*, Zondervan, 2003, or the article by Paul Copan, Does the Bible Teach Reincarnation? in *The Apologetics Study Bible*, Holman Bible Publishers, 2007.

[183.] Richard Dawkins, *The God Delusion*, W. F. Howes, 2006, p.373.

Now Richard Dawkins was voted one of the top three intellectuals in the world,[184] but you don't have to be one of the other two to answer his question, or any of the other questions that are sometimes raised about the death of Christ.

Why couldn't God just forgive?

Guillaume Bignon was an atheist. He met a girl who caught his attention, but there was just one problem – she was a Christian. Guillaume knew this was going to hinder his intentions, so he would have to disabuse her of her infantile beliefs. He didn't expect this to be a very difficult task, but he was in for a surprise. He investigated the Gospels, finding them to be historically reliable, and Jesus Christ to be captivating and compelling, but there was one question that he asked himself again and again – "Why did Jesus have to die?"

The answer came when God "reactivated my conscience." God showed him the seriousness of his sin, and it was then he realised why Jesus had to die. His sins had to be dealt with; justice had to be done.[185]

Greg Koukl recounts a conversation he had which makes the point:

> When I was speaking at a bookstore once, a lawyer came up to me and asked why Jesus was the only way. Instead of

---

[184.] The Prospect/FP Top 100 Public Intellectuals, October 2005.
[185.] http://www.theologui.blogspot.co.uk/2014/09/conversion-guillaume-bignon-french-atheist-to-christian-theologian.html.

answering directly, I asked him a question: "Do you believe
people who commit moral crimes ought to be punished?"

"Yes," he said.

"So do I," I responded.

Then I asked him, "Have you ever committed any moral crimes?"

"Yes," he said.

"So have I," I responded. "So now we have this difficult
situation. We both believe those who commit moral crimes
should be punished, and we both believe we've committed
moral crimes. Do you know what I call that? Bad news."

I continued, "This is where Jesus comes in. We both know
we're guilty, worthy of punishment. God offers a pardon on
His terms: Jesus, because He has personally paid the penalty
on our behalf. You can either take the pardon and go free, or
leave it and pay for your own crimes yourself."[186]

As we said in the previous chapter, if God is a God of
justice, then sin must be paid for. Being sorry for your sins
isn't a reason for you to escape the punishment. Indeed,
part and parcel of being sorry is recognising that you
deserve punishment. If someone has committed a crime
and is sincerely sorry, he doesn't say, "Well, there's no
need for me to turn myself in to the police, because I'm
sorry." No, because he's sorry he does turn himself in to
the police.

[186.] https://www.str.org/blog/why-is-jesus-the-only-way#.WWy_FdQrKt8.

So God could not forgive at the expense of *justice*, rather He forgave at the expense of *Jesus* – He gave His Son to pay the penalty, thus allowing God to offer forgiveness to the guilty and give it to the repentant.

How does His crucifixion pay for my sin?

People think that God was displaying wanton cruelty by having His Son violently executed, and they wonder how His crucifixion could atone for sin, given that crucifixion was a hideously barbaric invention of mankind.

The answer is found in recognising that the Lord Jesus was not merely bearing the physical pains of crucifixion. Many have experienced those pains, but none have experienced what Christ experienced when He was on the cross. As He hung there, He bore from God the judgment due to our sin. The crucifixion was man's action, displaying the sinfulness of the human heart, but when we were showing the depths of our hatred for God, God was showing the depths of His love for us, in that He laid on His Son the sin of a guilty world and punished Him for it. So His suffering for sin was not inflicted upon Him by men, but by God.

How come He only suffered for a few hours but we will suffer forever?

There was a young man hurling abuse at an open air preacher, and I approached him to find out what his problem was. He told me that he thought our message made no sense and was unfair. He said, "You believe that if

I'm not saved I'll go to hell forever, but Jesus only suffered for a few hours. Can I not get my suffering in a few hours like He did?"

The answer to his understandable question is found in seeing that sin carries an infinite penalty, which means that finite creatures like us can never pay it. Only an infinite person could pay an infinite penalty. So the Lord Jesus could pay what we could never pay, and He could say what we could never say – "It is finished."

Conclusion

Apart from the death of Christ the only way sins can be forgiven and sinners can be saved is if God compromises with sin and fudges on justice – an impossibility. Against the dark background of man's hatred and sin shine the bright rays of God's love and righteousness. We can glory in the cross and preach it with confidence, knowing that it is "to them that perish foolishness; but unto us which are saved it is the power of God" (1 Cor. 1:18, KJV).

4. The resurrection of Christ

Paul said that if Christ has not risen our faith is in vain and we are yet in our sins (1 Cor. 15:17). There is no salvation without a risen Christ.

One approach we can take to the subject of the resurrection is to show that the Bible is God's word, and it says He is risen. Sometimes the conversation doesn't allow this approach. In this section, we will look at another.

If you are talking to someone who takes the Bible to be nothing more than a collection of old books, that does not mean that what those books record is false,[187] and many of the significant claims and events can be demonstrated by the tools of the historian to be truly historical. J. N. Darby wrote:

> ... in reasoning with infidels ... I have sometimes done so on their own ground, to show how untenable their complaints, even setting aside inspiration. Indeed, did not the scriptures claim this authority, no one would dream of calling in question their authenticity or the evidence on which they rest.[188]

The evidence for the resurrection of Christ is a case in point.

There are many very helpful books on the evidence for the resurrection.[189] These works tend to set out the facts that are accepted by historians and show that the resurrection explains all these facts. They then show that naturalistic, non-miraculous explanations fail to account for the historical data. One weakness with this approach is that it allows sceptics to shrug their shoulders and say, "We just don't know what the explanation is." So there is a very

---

[187.] This is a point worth making to someone who tells you, *The Bible was written by men!* (As if you didn't know.) I like to ask them if they have any books that weren't written by men (or women), and if a human author necessarily means that what is written is false. They have to do more to disqualify the Bible than just point out that men wrote it.

[188.] J. N. Darby, *The Irrationalism of Infidelity*, preface, available freely at www.stempublishing.com.

[189.] For example, Gary R. Habermas & Michael R. Licona, *The Case for the Resurrection of Jesus*, Kregel Publications; the relevant chapters in Lee Strobel, *The Case for Christ, A Journalist's Personal Investigation of the Evidence for Jesus*, Zondervan; and Wright, *The Resurrection of the Son of God*.

simple approach that doesn't open that door to them. It can be expressed briefly, and only requires that the person you speak to agrees to one historical fact.

Step one – just one fact

The fact is this – *the disciples claimed to have been with the risen Christ*. Now this is not at all controversial. It has multiple, independent attestation, being mentioned in the Gospels,[190] the Acts,[191] the epistles[192] and in the very early creed of 1 Corinthians 15:3-7. And by saying that they *claimed* to have been with Him means that the person you are talking to is very likely to agree – he's not committing himself to anything miraculous.

Step two – just two options

The next step is even less controversial. They were either right or wrong about their claim. You should have no difficulty getting agreement there.

Step three – if they were wrong then ...

Step three involves looking at the option that they were wrong. There are only two ways they could have been

---

[190.] See footnote 174. The resurrection appearances in the Gospels are not legendary development or theological propaganda, but genuine eyewitness accounts of actual events.

[191.] Greek scholars have demonstrated that some of the sermon summaries in Acts, (e.g. Peter's in Acts 10) are written in "rough Greek" rather than in the usual style of Luke. This shows Luke wasn't putting words into the mouth of the preacher, but was summarising what the preacher actually said. See Habermas & Licona, *The Case for the Resurrection of Jesus*, 2004, p. 261, note 29.

[192.] Notice that (in 1 Cor. 9:1) Paul assumes that being an apostle entails seeing the risen Lord.

wrong – either they knew they were wrong or they did not know they were wrong. If they didn't know they were wrong then they were just mistaken. If they knew they were wrong then they were lying.

Then you examine each of those options.

Sincerely mistaken?

The problem is that the disciples didn't base their belief in the resurrection on a passing glimpse. They didn't say that one misty morning or one stormy night they saw someone down the street or across the road the same size and build as Jesus, and concluded He must be alive. No, their claim was that they were with Him on multiple occasions. The 1 Corinthians 15 creed lists many appearances to individuals and groups, believers and unbelievers (James and Paul), and to a group of over 500 at once, and Paul says most of them are still living – the implied challenge is "Go and ask them."[193] The Gospels and Acts independently agree with this creed and emphasise the physical nature of the appearances – His disciples handled the body, looked at the wounds, and had conversations and meals with Him.[194] This isn't something you can be sincerely mistaken about.

[193.] Hallucinations are first-person private events, like dreams. A group can't hallucinate the same thing. In addition, no matter how many hallucinations they had, they wouldn't get the body out of the tomb.

[194.] Resurrection to Jews and Gentiles meant nothing less than the reanimation of the body that had died (Jews believed there would be a resurrection at the last day, Gentiles did not; see Wright, *The Resurrection of the Son of God*). The disciples wouldn't have believed in the Lord's resurrection without tangible, physical proof. When they first saw the Lord, they "supposed they had seen a spirit" (Luke 24:37).

Deliberately lying?

Maybe they just made the whole thing up? There are (at least) three major problems with this.

i. The disciples weren't atheistic

As we said in regard to the deity of Christ, the first Christians were Jews. They proclaimed Jesus to be the Messiah, the Son of God, the means of salvation, the fulfilment of the Old Covenant, even though He had been crucified. If they made this up then they weren't apostles, they were apostates. If they weren't convinced that Jesus was living then they must have been convinced that God wasn't living, because their preaching would have been blasphemous if untrue.

ii. The disciples weren't idiotic

Why would they make up a message about a resurrection when it brought them no earthly gain? Their lie would have incurred the wrath of God and also the wrath of the Jewish and Roman authorities. Paul tells us in 1 Corinthians 4 about the power, prestige and wealth the apostles enjoyed:

> For I think that God hath set forth us the apostles last, as it were appointed to death: for we are made a spectacle unto the world, and to angels, and to men. We are fools for Christ's sake, but ye are wise in Christ; we are weak, but ye are strong; ye are honourable, but we are despised. Even unto this present hour we both hunger, and thirst, and are naked, and are buffeted, and have no certain dwellingplace; and labour,

*working with our own hands: being reviled, we bless; being
persecuted, we suffer it: being defamed, we intreat: we are
made as the filth of the world, and are the offscouring of all
things unto this day. (1 Cor. 4:9-13, KJV)*

People lie to get themselves out of trouble, not to get
themselves into trouble. No one suffers for something they
know to be false.

iii. The disciples weren't sadistic

It wasn't just the apostles who suffered for their message.
Those who believed it were led into lives of deprivation
and suffering. How cruel and heartless would someone
have to be to preach a lie that you knew, if believed, would
cause the believer to lose everything? Peter wrote to
suffering Christians to encourage them to keep on going.
He told them that they have a living hope because of the
resurrection (1 Pet. 1:3). Are we to suppose he was laughing
to himself thinking, "These fools believe this!"? Of course
not. These men were not cruel.

It is therefore inconceivable that these disciples made up
the story of the resurrection. They weren't liars.

Step four – they weren't wrong, so ...

It follows then that if they weren't mistaken and if they
weren't lying then they weren't wrong. And if they weren't
wrong then they were right – the Lord is risen indeed.

Step five – so what?

You can then draw out the significance of the resurrection:

i. It's God's seal of approval on who He is

The Lord Jesus claimed to be the Son of God. If He wasn't, then that was a blasphemous claim, meaning that God would not have raised Him, and He could not have raised Himself.

ii. It's God's stamp of authority on what He said

Because He is the Son of God then all that He taught comes with divine authority.

iii. It's God's sign of acceptance of what He did

He gave Himself to pay the penalty for sin. The resurrection is the proof that God is satisfied with the payment.

Here's a sample conversation to show you how you can use this approach.

- **Hello. We are having some meetings in your area and are letting people know about them. We would really love you to come along some evening.**

- What are they about?

- **They are about the Christian gospel and its relevance to us today.**

- I don't believe any of that.

- **Really? Why not?**

- There's no evidence for it.

- **Oh. Have you looked into it much?**

- Yeah.

- **What about the evidence for the resurrection of Christ?**

- What evidence?! There is none.

- **Well, I think there is. If you've looked into the subject then you will know that there's no doubt about this – the disciples claimed to have been with Christ after His resurrection.**

- Yes, they claimed to be.

- **Right. Now I think you'll agree with this next point too, they were either right or wrong.**

- Obviously.

- **Okay. So, if they were wrong then we have only two options: either they thought they were right and made a mistake, or they knew they were wrong and were telling lies. But neither of those options is remotely possible.**

- Why not?

- **Well, think about the option that they were mistaken. The thing is that these disciples didn't say that they caught a glimpse of someone who looked like Jesus. Their claim was that over a period of nearly six weeks they were in His company on** many occasions, listening to His teaching, eating meals with Him, looking at the wounds, handling the body. That's not something that you can be sincerely mistaken about. Would you agree?

- Right. So then they made it up.

- There are insurmountable problems with that option. First of all, if they were making this up then they had no fear of God, because they claimed that this man who was crucified was equal with God and worthy of worship. There's no way any God-fearing Jew would have made up such a story. And secondly, people make things up to gain something. All these men got for their story was persecution and pain. They were prepared to give their lives for it.

- But Muslim terrorists give their lives – that doesn't mean what they believe is true.

- No, but it means they believe it's true. If they knew it was false they wouldn't die for it. And if the disciples knew the resurrection was a hoax then they wouldn't be prepared to die for it. So they couldn't have been mistaken and they wouldn't have been lying, which means they weren't wrong. And if they weren't wrong, then they were right.

- Well, I don't believe it.

- That's your choice. But if you want to hold your view sensibly then you have to pick which option you are going with – did they think they were right or know they were wrong? There's no other option. Why would you not believe that their claim was true?

- Because dead people don't just get up and walk around! Science shows that dead people don't rise.

- Exactly, dead people don't rise naturally.[195] If they did then the resurrection wouldn't be much of a sign. But the disciples weren't claiming He naturally rose from the dead. They were claiming that God raised Him from the dead.

- It doesn't make any sense.

- What do you mean?

- It just seems impossible.

- It's only impossible if God doesn't exist, but if God exists then it all makes perfect sense. And I'll tell you what I think is impossible, that all these people got it wrong or all these people made it up and gave their lives for it. The only option that fits the facts is the one these disciples risked their lives and gave their lives proclaiming – He is risen. And another thing, I'm not just looking at history and coming to a conclusion – I've experienced the reality of Christ and His salvation in my life – I know that this is real. And if it's real

---

[195.] I sometimes like to point out here that science also shows that life doesn't come from non-life but that doesn't stop them believing it happened.

then it's something everyone needs. I would urge you to look at it seriously; it's far too important to dismiss.

Summary

Saul of Tarsus had it all. He was a strict adherent to the Mosaic covenant; he had prestige and respect amongst the Jewish community. This man was suddenly transformed. The man who gloried in his Jewish accomplishments changed his view and counted them as dung (Php. 3:4-9). The respected rabbi became a persecuted preacher. Christianity's chief antagonist became its greatest protagonist. What brought about the change? It was an encounter with the risen Christ. Paul knew full well what the stakes were – if he was wrong he had lost everything in this life for nothing, and he had lost everything in the life to come. But Paul wasn't nervous. His conversion to Christ wasn't a gamble. He wasn't wasting his life or risking his soul. Jesus Christ is risen – Paul had seen Him, he was sure of it, and we can be just as sure.

And if Christ is not risen, then our preaching is empty and your faith is also empty. Yes, and we are found false witnesses of God, because we have testified of God that He raised up Christ, whom He did not raise up — if in fact the dead do not rise. For if the dead do not rise, then Christ is not risen. And if Christ is not risen, your faith is futile; you are still in your sins! Then also those who have fallen asleep in Christ have perished. If in this life only we have hope in Christ, we are of all men the most pitiable.

But now Christ is risen from the dead ... (1 Cor. 15:14-20)

Conclusion

When Philip told Nathanael he had found the Messiah, Nathanael was more than a bit sceptical. He had presuppositions that made it impossible for him to believe that Jesus of Nazareth could be who Philip said He was. Philip's response was "Come and see." He knew that if he could get Nathanael to look honestly and listen carefully to Jesus then he would come to the same conclusion, and he was right. Nathanael saw something in Jesus that led him to confess Him as the Son of God (John 1:45-49). We have the same responsibility as Philip to call people to come and see, and we have the same privilege of introducing people to the Messiah. It is our prayer that this chapter will have given you some useful resources to do just that, and may it be that God will grant you will have the same joy Philip had – the joy of seeing someone come to recognise who Jesus really is, and believe in Him.

Conclusion

Spurgeon said, "Do you want to go to heaven alone? I fear you will never go there. Have you no wish for others to be saved? Then you are not saved yourself. Be sure of that."[196]

Stirring words. They make us eager to evangelise, but they don't make it easy.

We have known what it's like to have heard a challenging sermon and emerge full of courage and enthusiasm only to shrink away in terror at the smell of conflict. We have often returned from the evangelistic battlefield without having fired a shot. We know the feeling of being bruised and battered after an encounter. Have you been there? What do you do?

The US Marines have a saying, "The more you sweat in training, the less you bleed in battle." This book contains some of the training we have found really helpful. It has been tested in battle and it works. It has enabled us to manoeuvre around obstacles, avoid traps and demolish defences, so that many people have heard the gospel. We recognise that methods, tactics and apologetics don't

---

[196.] http://www.spurgeongems.org/vols34-36/chs2019.pdf.

save. The Lord saves, but if we want to see the Lord work in salvation through us then we need to get involved in spreading the message. Our aim in writing this book is that you would not only be more enthused to evangelise but more equipped, and that you would have the awesome privilege of seeing the Lord at work. He's willing to use you. Are you willing to be used?

RECOMMENDED READING

If you wish to explore the subjects of this book in more detail, we would recommend the following publications. Inclusion on this list is not an unqualified endorsement but simply a recognition that we have found the book beneficial.

Books marked with * are at a more advanced or scholarly level rather than a popular level.

On Evangelism

General

Jerram Barrs, *The Heart of Evangelism*, InterVarsity Press, 2001.

Kenneth Fleming, *Essentials of Missionary Service: Studies in Paul's Missionary Strategy*, OM Publishing, 2000.

*Michael Green, *Evangelism in the Early Church*, Eagle, Inter Publishing Service, 1995.

Peter Jeffery, *How shall they hear?: Church-based evangelism,* Evangelical Press, 1996.

Kenneth Prior, *The Gospel in a Pagan Society,* Christian Focus Publications, 1995.

W. E. Vine, *The Divine Plan of Missions,* Pickering & Inglis Ltd.

Personal

Jerram Barrs, *Learning Evangelism from Jesus,* Crossway Books, 2009.

James Boccardo, *Unsilenced: How to Voice the Gospel,* CrossBooks, 2010.

Joe Carter & John Coleman, *How to Argue like Jesus: Learning Persuasion from History's Greatest Communicator,* Crossway, 2009.

Ray Comfort, *The Way of the Master,* Bridge-Logos, 2006.

Mark Dever, *The Gospel and Personal Evangelism,* Crossway Books, 2007.

Douglas Groothuis, *On Jesus, Wadsworth Philosophers Series,* Wadsworth Cengage Learning, 2003.

Os Guinness, *Fool's Talk: recovering the art of Christian persuasion,* InterVarsity Press, 2015.

Gregory Koukl, *Tactics: A game plan for discussing your Christian convictions,* Zondervan, 2009.

John S. Leonard, *Get Real: Sharing your Everyday Faith Every Day*, New Growth Press, 2013.

Paul E. Little, *How to Give Away Your Faith*, InterVarsity Press, 2007.

Randy Newman, *Questioning Evangelism: Engaging People's Hearts the Way Jesus Did*, Kregel, 2017.

Rico Tice with Carl Laferton, *Honest Evangelism: How to talk about Jesus even when it's tough*, The Good Book Company, 2015.

Paul Williams, *Intentional: Evangelism That Takes People To Jesus*, 10Publishing, 2016.

On Apologetics

General

John Blanchard, *Does God Believe in Atheists?*, Evangelical Press, 2000.

William Lane Craig, *On Guard: Defending your Faith with Reason and Precision*, David C. Cook, 2010.

*William Lane Craig, *Reasonable Faith: Christian Truth and Apologetics*, Third Edition, Crossway, 2008.

Norman L. Geisler & Frank Turek, *I Don't Have Enough Faith to Be an Atheist*, Crossway, 2004.

Norman L. Geisler, *The Big Book of Christian Apologetics: An A to Z Guide*, Baker Books, 2012.

*Douglas Groothuis, *Christian Apologetics: A Comprehensive Case for Biblical Faith*, InterVarsity Press, 2011.

Timothy Keller, *The Reason for God: Belief in an age of scepticism*, Hodder & Stoughton, 2008.

John C. Lennox, *Gunning for God: Why the New Atheists are Missing the Target*, Lion Hudson, 2011.

C. S. Lewis, *Mere Christianity*, HarperCollins, 2002.

Lee Strobel, *The Case for Faith: A Journalist Investigates the Toughest Objections to Christianity*, Zondervan, 2000.

Frank Turek, *Stealing from God: Why atheists need God to make their case*, NavPress, 2014.

Scripture

Paul Copan, *Is God a Moral Monster?: Making Sense of the Old Testament God*, Baker Books, 2011.

Paul McCauley, *Prove It: How you can know and show that the Bible is God's word*, Decapolis Press, 2017.

Josh McDowell & Sean McDowell, *Evidence that Demands a Verdict: Life-Changing Truth for a Sceptical World*, Authentic, 2017.

R. C. Newman (ed.), *The Evidence of Prophecy*, Interdisciplinary Biblical Research Institute.

Science

Edgar Andrews, *Who Made God?: Searching for a theory of everything*, EP Books, 2009.

Lee Strobel, *The Case for a Creator: A Journalist Investigates Scientific Evidence That Points toward God*, Zondervan, 2004.

J. Warner Wallace, *God's Crime Scene: A Cold-Case Detective Examines the Evidence for a Divinely Created Universe*, David C. Cook, 2015.

Suffering

Francis J. Beckwith & Gregory Koukl, *Relativism: Feet Firmly Planted in Mid-Air*, Baker Books, 1998.

C. S. Lewis, *The Problem of Pain*, HarperCollins, 1996.

Salvation

Paul Copan & Kenneth D. Litwak, *The Gospel in the Marketplace of Ideas: Paul's Mars Hill Experience for Our Pluralistic World*, IVP, 2014.

Timothy Keller, *Making Sense of God: An Invitation to the Sceptical*, Hodder & Stoughton, 2016.

The Saviour

Lee Strobel, *The Case for Christ: A Journalist's Personal Investigation of the Evidence for Jesus*, Zondervan, 2016.

Lee Strobel, *The Case for the Real Jesus: A Journalist Investigates Current Attacks on the Identity of Christ*, Zondervan, 2014.

J. Warner Wallace, *Cold-Case Christianity: A Homicide Detective investigates the claims of the Gospels*, David C Cook, 2013.